Cultivating a Contemplative Heart
and Becoming a Person of Prayer

Cultivating a Contemplative Heart *and Becoming a* Person *of* Prayer

Mary Beth Kremski

Our Sunday Visitor
Huntington, Indiana

Nihil Obstat
Msgr. Michael Heintz, Ph.D.
Censor Librorum

Imprimatur
✠ Kevin C. Rhoades
Bishop of Fort Wayne-South Bend
May 12, 2025

The *Nihil Obstat* and *Imprimatur* are official declarations that a book is free from doctrinal or moral error. It is not implied that those who have granted the *Nihil Obstat* and *Imprimatur* agree with the contents, opinions, or statements expressed.

30 29 28 27 26 25 1 2 3 4 5 6 7 8 9

Our Sunday Visitor Publishing Division
Our Sunday Visitor, Inc.
200 Noll Plaza
Huntington, IN 46750
www.osv.com
1-800-348-2440

ISBN: 978-1-63966-316-3 (Inventory No. T2964)
1. RELIGION—Christianity—Catholic.
2. RELIGION—Christian Living—Prayer.
3. RELIGION—Christian Living—Spiritual Growth.

eISBN: 978-1-63966-317-0
LCCN: 2025942778

Cover design: Tyler Ottinger
Cover art: *Christ in the House of Martha and Mary*, Alamy Images
Interior design: Amanda Falk

PRINTED IN THE UNITED STATES OF AMERICA

This book is dedicated to Saint Joseph, faithful father and guardian of contemplatives, and to my husband, Stan — no words are enough.

Contents

Introduction

"I came to cast fire upon the earth ..."
— Luke 12:49

The greatest thing you can do with your life is cultivate a contemplative heart. You may question that claim, but I'm confident that by the end of this book, you'll be convinced. What is a contemplative heart? Let me answer that question by first looking at the word *heart.*

Lest anyone think that *heart* is a superficial, sentimental word, consider what the *Catechism of the Catholic Church* has to say about it: "The heart is the dwelling-place where I am, where I live. ... The heart is the place 'to which I withdraw.' The heart is our hidden center ... the place of decision ... the place of encounter. ... It is the *heart* that prays" (CCC 2563).

But what is a *contemplative* heart? Maybe we should begin

with what it's not. You don't have to regularly (or ever) fall into ecstasy or see visions to have a contemplative heart. You don't have to be faultless or spend endless hours a day in prayer. Neither do you have to live behind monastery walls or wear a religious habit to be a truly contemplative person. Of course, for those who are called to contemplative religious life, the enclosure of a monastery is a necessary part of their vocation. But even those of us who do not live in a monastery can live a contemplative life. That's because God doesn't judge us by external factors. He looks at the heart. And what's essential to contemplative life is found in the heart.

Now that we know what a contemplative heart *isn't,* let's turn our attention to what it is! As you progress through the book, you'll discover many beautiful qualities of a contemplative heart, but its primary identifying characteristic is a passionate love for God — a longing to be with him, to listen to him, to belong to him. These longings naturally result in a desire for prayer and for a close interior relationship with God that leads to a loving obedience to him.

The contemplative is captivated by the knowledge that God dwells within her soul — "Do you not know that you are God's temple and that God's Spirit dwells in you?" (1 Cor 3:16). And she is irresistibly drawn to seek him there. Like Moses who stopped to notice the burning bush, the contemplative focuses her gaze on the sanctuary of her soul, as if to say: "I will turn aside and see this great sight" (Ex 3:3). And like Moses, she encounters the living God.

Through faith in his presence within her, she makes real contact with the Lord. If she is faithful to prayer, her conscious awareness of God's presence within her heart will continue to grow. When, at times, she has no felt sense of God's presence, she knows with the assurance of faith that he is still abiding in her soul.

This emphasis on seeking God within your heart might make you think contemplative spirituality is self-centered when exactly the opposite is true. The Church has consistently promoted contemplative life as a powerful means of bringing Christ to souls and to the world. In an interview with Paul Senz of *Catholic World Report,* Fr. Donald Haggerty sums up the reason: "Hidden contemplative souls are the great fire burning beneath all that is fruitful in the Church. … Contemplative souls have a unique power of intercession for others precisely because they are souls of love."

If you desire this fire of divine love to burn within your heart, know that this very desire is "the beginning of love" (CCC 2709). And this book is intended to help you fan it into flame! Even if you are not quite sure yet, but you have some desire for a greater life of prayer, ask God to give you this desire.

This desire to love God passionately, and to be filled with his love, is often a sign of a call to contemplative spirituality — whether in religious life or in the world. It was for me. Despite my many faults, I've had a hunger for God almost as far back as I can remember. It manifested in different ways — persistent seeking to know the purpose of life, a need to belong to God, an attraction to the interior life. I didn't understand these longings, nor what God was trying to say to me through them, until I came across the book *The Story of a Soul,* which is the autobiography of the Carmelite nun St. Thérèse of Lisieux.

Through her book, I discovered that there is a path to holiness open to people who aren't hankering for martyrdom but who struggle simply to navigate the demands of daily life — little people, like me. And I finally understood my spiritual identity: contemplative. I particularly resonated with Carmelite contemplative spirituality. This is why you will notice throughout this book that I've referenced Carmelite sources more than those of other spiritual traditions. But you don't have to be a Carmelite to be a contemplative! There are many other spiritual traditions that have contemplative branches, including Dominicans, Franciscans, and the Missionaries of Charity, just to name a few.

And if you're not attracted to any of these, that's fine. You don't need a label to be a contemplative. Remember, God knows who you are — by your heart.

This invitation, to be a contemplative, to live a life of deep prayer is not reserved for the very holy or for those in religious life. Rather, as Fr. Jacques Philippe reminds us in his excellent book *Time for God*, "The call to prayer, to the mystical life, to union with God in prayer is as universal as the call to holiness." If you want your soul to be a sanctuary filled with God's presence, even in the midst of your busy life with its endless lists and unfinished tasks, you already have the beginnings of a contemplative heart. The ongoing formation of your contemplative heart will make it possible for you to live with an ever-growing awareness of God's presence — which is a deep form of prayer — even as you deal with the demands of your day.

So resolve to offer to God your desire, combined with your small, persistent efforts, and he will run to meet you with his grace. For it's God's grace, his power and life at work within you, that fashions your heart into a contemplative heart — a heart that is transformed by his presence "from one degree of glory to another" (2 Cor 3:18). Glory is just another way of saying union with God, oneness with his presence, conformity with his character.

Just consider: If you seek a contemplative heart, you'll be pursuing the true meaning of life: union with God in love. You'll open yourself to the Source of the joy "no one will take" from you (Jn 16:22) and the love that's worth more than all the treasures of the world. A contemplative heart will become for you a font of peace and strength. And if you choose to embark on this journey, I promise, you'll never be bored!

While not an in-depth treatise on contemplative prayer (classics old and new have already been written on that subject, including works by St. Teresa of Ávila, St. John of the Cross, and Fr. Thomas Dubay, whose books are readily available), this book is designed to prepare you to receive both the gift of a contemplative heart and the grace of contemplative prayer. Drawing upon the wisdom of the saints and other faithful spiritual writers, with a few of my own spiritual adventures thrown in, it will explain the qualities of a contemplative heart and how they can be yours.

Each chapter will reveal a little more of the "anatomy" of a contemplative heart.

First, we will see that a contemplative heart is centered on Jesus. Your relationship with Jesus is the source of all the graces needed for your contemplative journey. A common mistake is to inadvertently look past him as we set our sights on "loftier" spiritual goals. But we *never* outgrow Jesus. On the contrary, we grow when our gaze is fixed on him. Chapter 1 offers encouragement to remember him always, and his amazing love for you.

Second, a contemplative heart hungers for truth. Neither love nor contemplation can exist apart from truth. A contemplative heart feeds on spiritual truth, but even when we have decided to follow the truth, we may not be aware of some inner hindrances that are preventing us from hearing and accepting truth in its fullness. Chapter 2 will explore some of the more common obstacles to hearing truth so that we can be freed from them and be given "ears to hear" all that Jesus wants to say to us. We will also highlight some of the treasures of our Faith and briefly explore why we believe what we believe. This exercise will strengthen our faith so that it can withstand the tempests of our times. Truth can only have its full effect in our lives when we see it clearly and believe it firmly. In Chapter 2, you'll learn why we should believe in the Catholic Church — despite the scandals, despite the hurts that may have come to us from Church leaders and other Catholics, despite everything!

Next, a contemplative heart listens to the voice of God. As you grow in your love for God, you will inevitably grow in your desire to do his will. Chapter 3 will unpack how you can come to recognize God's voice and understand some ways he may be speaking to you. As you discover and follow God's will through listening to his voice, you will grow in union with him.

A contemplative heart is a missionary heart that knows the value of prayer. In Chapter 4, we'll examine the question of the "usefulness" of prayer — in particular, contemplative prayer, which on the outside appears to be doing nothing. When you become convinced of the worth of prayer, your whole life will find new meaning.

A contemplative heart loves the hidden life, as Chapter 5 will explore. Is a hidden life possible outside of the monastery? The truth is, not only is it possible, but also no matter where it's lived, a hidden life in imitation of Jesus and Mary is filled with spiritual treasure and deep contentment.

A contemplative heart longs for union with the Bridegroom. All of us who are baptized (men and women alike) are called to a deep, spousal union with Jesus. But is this possible for all of us? Or is spiritual marriage with Christ reserved for those in the priesthood and religious life? As laypeople, we've received mixed messages on this issue. In Chapter 6, you'll find answers to this and other related questions.

Suffering will be part of each of our lives, and rather than rejecting this, a contemplative heart views suffering in the light of the cross. Sharing in the heart of Jesus means sharing in his suffering. Chapter 7 will discuss how to carry your cross with greater peace, and how to make the most of it for yourself and for God's kingdom. Here, we'll specifically focus on physical suffering, but physical suffering inevitably impacts other areas.

Closely related to suffering is the call to surrender. A contemplative heart lives a surrendered life. In Chapter 8, we'll witness the power of surrender to bring peace and union with God in the midst of situations we feel are over our heads. How can a surrendered, contemplative heart help you keep your balance and even go forward through difficulties in ways you never expected?

Finally, a contemplative heart looks to Mary. In Chapter 9, Mary is presented as the perfect model of a contemplative heart. Keeping the icon of Mary's heart before your eyes and looking to her for support will keep you on the right path. In addition, examining the themes of previous chapters in the light of Mary's example will provide you with a mini-digest of our contemplative lessons. When you learn from Mary the value of a contemplative heart, I guarantee you won't want to exchange it for anything in the world!

As you seek a heart of prayer through the pages of this book, know that you will be remembered in my prayers, just as you are certainly held in the prayers of our Mother Mary.

Mary, Queen and Mother of Contemplatives, pray for us!

Chapter 1
Remember Jesus

"Apart from me you can do nothing."
— John 15:5

The essence and driving force of a contemplative heart is devotion to the Person of Jesus Christ. Of course, I'm not excluding the Father and the Holy Spirit. The reality is that Jesus is the Way to the Father in the Holy Spirit, so it is through Jesus that we enter the life of the Holy Trinity. Our relationship with Jesus is the one thing necessary (see Lk 10:42), as he told Saint Martha. He is the essential foundation upon which every authentic contemplative life must be built (1 Cor 3:10–11). Thus it is important that we take the time and effort specifically to *remember* him.

Remembering is important to God, and vital for us. It's a theme that runs through Scripture. Over and over again, the Lord calls us to "remember the wonderful works that he has done" (Ps 105:5). To remember his greatness and his merciful love. Why? Is it because he's insecure and needs us to bolster his ego? No. It's because *we're* insecure and easily forget his infinite love for us and his presence with us. And God knows that when his people forget him, they drift.

Remembering is also central to the identity of the contemplative soul because a contemplative is called to live with an ever-greater awareness, or remembrance, of the presence of God. We are to be attentive to him, as much as God's grace and our ability to respond allows.

And isn't remembering the instinctual response of one who loves? Think of when you first fell in love, or when you had a new baby in the house. Did you struggle to remember your beloved or the little one waiting at home for you? Did you get bored or tired of thinking about them? Or could you have said with the poet Samuel Taylor Coleridge, "And in life's noisiest hour there whispers still the ceaseless love of thee"? In the midst of the world's noise, we still experience a continuous current of love and remembrance.

How much more, then, should we remember Jesus — the One who is our life and who abides with us continually? He is always thinking of us. Let's at least make the intention of remembering him often throughout the day. His grace will help us to carry it out.

Admittedly, it's not easy to maintain that level of attentiveness for the long haul. The burdens, fears, and stresses of life can wear us down, even overwhelm us. Our memory and our love become dulled. To keep them vibrant, they must be perpetually renewed by our deliberate decision.

I don't know what condition you're in as you read this book, but I think it's safe to assume that you, like all of us, are a bit tattered (like the Velveteen Rabbit by the end of the old children's story). We're worn out by the pace of life and anxious about the rising cost of living. Old hurts seem to rise up when we least expect them. We worry about our children or are overwhelmed by the needs of our aging parents. Or both! We need to turn to Jesus again and again. To remember his love and respond with ours. If we do this, we can be sure that our quest for a contemplative heart will be established on the one and only foundation that won't let us down, the one and only foundation that can support us in the storms of life — Jesus Christ.

Remember Me?

St. Teresa of Ávila said, "The failure to realize Someone is there, that God is there, lies at the root of all our problems in prayer. We will not do with him what we expect others to do with us when they speak to us — look at him." In other words, our problems with prayer stem from our failure to recognize that prayer is a relationship with a real Person who is present to us.

Similarly, the root cause of spiritual forgetfulness is a failure to realize that our spiritual life is not a task, but a relationship with a real, living Person, who longs for our company and our love, and who loves us beyond our desires.

So, think of remembering not like remembering where you put your keys, but in the context of relationship. Remembering is an expression of love. Don't you feel loved when someone thinks of you? Conversely, you know the pain that comes with feeling forgotten or overlooked. So does Jesus. And because he loves more, his pain is deeper.

In hopes of sharpening our spiritual memory, let's look at a few examples of how we might forget Jesus. The goal here is not to fill you with guilt, but to inspire you to grow in your devotion. Keep in mind, to acknowledge our failings is to stand in a place of grace — and transformation. So, don't be discouraged if you recognize yourself in the list below. (We're probably all there somewhere.) Instead, allow whatever insight you gain to make you more sensitive to the person of Jesus Christ.

We forget Jesus when:

- **We take him for granted.** We don't notice, acknowledge, or thank him for himself, or for the gifts he gives us every day. (But we rarely forget to complain!)
- **We don't share our life with him.** We "say our prayers," but we don't share our hearts. Or we keep our religious life — Jesus — separate from the rest of our life. We forget that Jesus is with us and wants to help us with *everything*. That he loves us always, even when we sin.
- **We're not interested in him.** We're not interested in learning more about the Lord. We rarely, if ever, meditate on Scripture. We're not spiritually hungry.
- **We don't give him quality time.** Our prayer is usually done "on the fly." We make no real effort to have a personal prayer time. (Everyone has crises and busy times when prayer suffers, and Jesus understands that. This is different — this is when prayer is consistently a low priority for us, and rarely offered from our heart.)
- **We fail to recognize him in the sacraments.** For example, we walk into the church without acknowledging the presence of Jesus in the tabernacle. We don't talk to him after we receive him in the Holy Eucharist. Our Lord is present and active in each of the sacraments. But do we recognize him there? By virtue of the Sacrament of Matrimony, Jesus is with you and your spouse, continually offering his

grace. In fact, all the grace you'll ever need to live your marriage well is available to you. Have you ever thought, for example, to ask him for the grace to understand your spouse? In the Sacrament of Penance, Jesus is there. He's the one who forgives your sin and heals your wounds. In each of the sacraments, Jesus is present, but do we remember his presence? Do we ask for his grace?

- **We don't remember he's dwelling within us.** We forget, or maybe never heard, that if we're baptized and in a state of grace, the Holy Trinity — God! — dwells within us. And so, we don't commune with him in our souls. We leave him alone.
- **We listen to others — including the media — more than to Jesus.** A very modern way to forget Jesus is to fill our hearts and minds with an abundance of media — even good media — which can drown him out. It's a matter of priorities and prudence. To whom do we listen most?
- **We substitute religious works for relationship.** Here's a personal illustration. I once had a dream in which I was in the sanctuary of a church. Members of the parish were engaged in various church works, laughing and talking. Jesus stood before me wearing a crown of gold woven with thorns, and a deeply sad expression. He was forgotten, overlooked by the very ones who sought to serve him. I began to shout, "Jesus is here! He's here!" But no one paid attention. Good work is good, but we must be careful not to forget Jesus in the process.

NOTE: Those seeking a contemplative heart are particularly vulnerable to these next two.

- **We become preoccupied with our spiritual progress.** We're preoccupied with our level of progress in prayer. Are we in the illuminative way? Which of St. Teresa of Ávila's seven mansions can we call home? Have we reached union? All of this puts the focus on ourselves and takes it off Jesus. Even in prayer, we can forget him!
- **We seek to advance beyond Jesus.** We seek experiences in prayer rather than seeking Christ through prayer. St. Teresa of Ávila and St. John of the Cross both warned against this error. If your prayer life has left Jesus behind, it has veered off course! Better check the map — God's word. It will tell you that Jesus is the source of *all* spiritual treasures.

I hope our little memory review will inspire you to think of Jesus more often and with greater attentiveness. Did one or two of the reminders listed above prick your conscience a bit? Which made you want to remember Jesus more? The answers to these questions are clues revealing where the Holy Spirit desires to work in your heart. And where the Holy Spirit gives light, he also gives grace. He will inspire you and enlighten you, little by little, a step at a time.

Another way to keep your memory sharp and your love fervent is to look, as if for the first time, at the Good News of what God has done for you in Jesus Christ. And then: take it personally!

Take It Personally

"I bring you good news of a great joy!" (Lk 2:10). This is how the angel announced the birth of Jesus to the shepherds. Are you experiencing that joy? Maybe, but maybe the bad news that comes at all of us every day has dimmed the light of the Good News for you. That's why we need to meditate on the Good News in some way every day.

What is this Good News? Consider: God, the eternal Creator of the universe, the second Person of the Blessed Trinity, humbled himself, took on a human nature, and walked the streets of this world — for you. He lived for you. He died for you. He rose for you. That's how deeply he wants to share his life and joy with you. And he's coming back — *for you.* (Please re-read that slowly.)

Jesus Christ willingly took the consequences of our sins upon himself on the Cross to snatch us from hell and claim us for heaven. "Christ Jesus came ... to save sinners" (1 Tm 1:15). If we acknowledge our sin and trust in the saving life and death of Jesus Christ, we will receive all the blessings of redemption. As the *Catechism* teaches, "Jesus knew and loved us each and all during his life, his agony, and his Passion and gave himself up for each one of us: 'The Son of God ... loved me and gave himself for me'" (478).

If we seriously considered the miraculous happenings that make up the basic message of the Gospel and the love that lies behind them, we'd be filled with wonder and joy. The Incarnation. The virgin birth. The God-man offering his own life. The Resurrection, which awaits all who believe. The gift of the Holy Spirit. And eternal life! (And for those of us watching ourselves age, more good news: We'll be young again!)

But haven't we gotten used to hearing these amazing facts? We've become bored with miracles. As Fr. Sean Davidson writes in his book *Saint Mary Magdalene: Prophetess of Eucharistic Love*, "God is revealing himself to the world in the Person of Jesus Christ, but few are the souls ... who give the Word of God the attention he deserves." I once read a story of a young Dutch missionary who shared the gospel message with an elderly man who had lived his whole life under Communism. The old man was "thunderstruck" and began weeping for joy, saying, "If only ... if only I'd known."

Are you — am I — thunderstruck with amazement at what God has done for us? Ask the Holy Spirit to awaken you to wonder, to help you realize it's all real and it's all *for you.* For "how shall we escape if we neglect such a great salvation" (Heb 2:3)?

Be amazed that you've been chosen "before the foundation of the world" to be "holy and blameless" (Eph 1:4). Overflow with thanksgiving that God has delivered you from the "dominion of darkness" and transferred you "to the kingdom of his beloved Son" (Col 1:13), and that Jesus is preparing a place in heaven *especially for you.*

But wait a minute! What does Scripture mean by "the dominion of darkness"? The reality is that all humanity, apart from the salvation of Jesus, is under the dominion of darkness — Satan and the demons, the wicked powers of the world, the oppression of our fallen nature, and our personal sins. It is a soul-crushing burden, and left to ourselves, we're stuck. Only the redemptive death of Jesus, the perfect Lamb of God, who took upon himself the devastating weight of all that darkness— and conquered it — can rescue us. Truly, "there is salvation in no one else" (Acts 4:12).

Regarding those who have never heard of Jesus, the Catholic Church tells us: "Those also can attain to salvation who through no fault of their own do not know the Gospel of Christ or His Church, yet sincerely seek God and moved by grace strive by their deeds to do His will" (*Lumen Gentium* 16). Seeing their sincere hearts and determined efforts, God imparts grace. But even here, Jesus is the source of this grace and of their salvation.

Why has Jesus saved us? Because of his incomprehensible love. The heartbroken Father wants his children back. Jesus aches for his Bride. The Holy Spirit longs to make your heart his home. But God can't save us unless we want to be saved. Unless we know we need to be saved. And unless we respond. (If you've never explicitly told Jesus that you believe in him, acknowledged your need to be forgiven, and offered your life to him, consider doing it now. If you have, there's no harm in telling him again.)

It's difficult for us to grasp a love like this. Harder to believe in it. Even St. Teresa of Calcutta had this concern for her religious sisters. Listen to what she wrote to them in her well-known Varanasi Letter, and *take it personally*:

> Jesus wants me to tell you again how much love he has for each one of you — beyond all you can imagine. I worry some of you have not really met Jesus — one to one — you and Jesus alone. … Have you seen with the eyes of your soul how He looks at you with love? Do you really know the living Jesus … ? Ask for the grace. He is longing to give it. … He misses you when you don't come close. He thirsts for you.

If we could see that look of infinite love in Jesus' eyes, would we ever forget him?

Contemplative Remembering

Contemplative remembering is a kind of prayer that seeks living contact with God through loving attentiveness to his presence — in prayer, in his word, in the circumstances of our lives, and within our hearts. "The Fathers of the spiritual life … insist that prayer is a remembrance of God often awakened by the memory of the heart: 'We must remember God more often than we draw breath'" (CCC 2697).

But this kind of remembering is no mere recollection. It's a living experience — one we enter into most fully in the holy sacrifice of the Mass. In the Mass, the life, death, resurrection, and ascension of Jesus Christ are made present to us, not merely by way of our memory, but by a miracle of the Holy Spirit, which makes it possible for us to truly be there, with Jesus. And when we are aware of this, when we are present to Jesus and these awesome realities, we will experience a real encounter with the Lord. If we don't make an effort to remember, to see with spiritual eyes what is happening in the Mass, we may be overcome by sleepiness, or distraction, or the woman sitting in front of us with the big hat!

We can also have a real encounter with Jesus at any time in our prayer. When, in faith, we turn to Jesus or meditate on his word, we touch a present reality. We make real contact with him. As Fr. Wojciech Giertych, OP, writes in his book *The Spark of Faith*, "When there is a moment of faith, when the believer consciously focuses his mind toward God [that is, remembers him] ... there is a direct contact with the mysterious but living God."

The more your mind is filled with the presence, words, and actions of God, the more it will be renewed through this contact with him. This can happen in a brief moment when you recall he is with you, or in pockets of time you use to read a bit of his word. In these brief encounters, God is powerfully at work.

St. Teresa of Ávila encourages us not to limit our remembering of God's presence and actions to the accounts recorded in the Bible, but to remember the great things he has done for us personally. When we do, we are renewing and deepening the graces God has given us and opening the door to new graces. St. Thérèse of Lisieux's classic autobiography, *The Story of a Soul,* is an example of exactly this type of remembering. Not only did she derive grace for herself from reliving the Lord's mercies toward her, but a perpetual stream of grace still flows from her pen. St. Augustine of Hippo, in his classic work *Confessions,* similarly meditates on God's great work in his life and, in the process, provides a treasury of spiritual wisdom for the ages.

Try this yourself. Ask the Holy Spirit to remind you of what the Lord has done for you over the years — gifts he has given you, lessons and lights. You will grow in gratitude and in the ability to notice and appreciate God's active presence in your life. Eventually, you'll discover that, as the Benedictine monk who wrote the book *In Sinu Jesu* expresses it, "nothing in your life escapes [his] attention." I strongly recommend making this remembering of the good things God has done for you a daily exercise. You may find Fr. Timothy Gallagher's book *The Examen Prayer* to be helpful for making this part of your daily life.

Another form of contemplative remembering is remembering as reparation. You remember Jesus for those who forget him, who are indifferent to him. St. Elizabeth of the Trinity, writing to Jesus about the social functions she was obliged to attend before entering Carmel, said, "At these reunions where no one is thinking of you, it seems to me that you are happy that there is one heart, even one so poor and feeble as mine, that does not forget you!" Resolve to be the one "poor" heart thinking of Jesus in places where he's forgotten.

To practice contemplative remembering in whatever form — through the Mass, through contact with God by faith, through his word, in your personal remembrance, or by offering reparation — is to imitate the prayer of Mary, whose "characteristic attitude," as Fr. Sean Davidson describes it, is that of "attentiveness to Jesus Christ. She is constantly pondering in her heart whatever Jesus says and does."

This is a very important statement because it tells us that contemplative remembering, contemplative prayer of any kind, is not merely an experience. It's not imagination or fantasy. Contemplative prayer is captivated by, and focused upon, truth, most especially the One who is Truth — Jesus Christ.

If that's the case, then to have a contemplative heart, we must feed on truth. We must love truth and seek it. We will explore this love for truth in the next chapter.

Make It Your Own

Ponder: Ponder the Nicene Creed. I suggest reading it slowly, whether in a missal or online. Try to read it as if you were learning of these amazing events for the first time. It's a greater love story than *Romeo and Juliet*, a more heroic tale than the *Lord of the Rings*, with a happy ending infinitely more wonderful than any fairy tale. And it's true! It matters to God that you don't miss it. He planned these gifts for you from all eternity.

Pray: Ask for the grace to know Jesus' individual love for you in a powerful and personal way. Ask him to help you see that look of infinite love — meant just for you — in his eyes, and to believe in his love for you. Sit quietly with him for a few minutes after you pray.

Practice: Make "remembering Jesus" a regular part of your everyday life, in your prayer and activities. Let him know he's welcome in every part of your life. Take some time to remember and note some of the special graces he has given you — things he's done for you, prayers he's answered. Thank him. Know that the more you do this, the more you will grow in trust.

Chapter 2
Love Truth

"I am the way, and the truth, and the life."
— John 14:6

Real love cannot exist apart from truth. A contemplative heart seeks to be filled with the love and presence of God, but this desire can only be fulfilled when we also seek truth. In fact, Saint Peter tells us it is by "obedience to the truth" (1 Pt 1:22) that our souls are purified and made capable of sincere love.

In his book *The Contemplative Hunger*, Fr. Donald Haggerty confirms that truth "is a necessity without which no contemplative life has ever been lived." Yes, God is love, but he is also truth. Didn't Jesus tell us that he is the truth (see Jn 14:6)? So, love for truth is love for God.

Common sense tells us we can't create or destroy spiritual reality by the power of our subjective, personal preferences. Truth is objective. Either God exists, or he doesn't. Heaven and hell are real, or they're not. Our beliefs, opinions, and preferences can't change what *is* — what's *true*. If we want to come to know and love God, we have to be intellectually honest, and that means accepting that truth can never be subjective. This reality is foundational to any sane — and saintly — life.

What did Jesus say about the importance and reality of spiritual truth?

True to His Word

What a blessing it is to be able to know with assurance what Jesus said about truth. His words have been recorded by the authors of the New Testament and preserved by the Church. As a faithful Christian, you probably have no problem believing that the New Testament is a reliable record of Jesus' life and teachings. But in the world, and even among Christians, this belief will encounter opposition, which could possibly raise a doubt in your mind — a doubt that could hinder your faith. So, let's briefly take a look at some historical evidence that supports the reliability of the New Testament.

Scholars have applied the same tests of historical accuracy to the New Testament that have been applied to other ancient documents and have found it to be very reliable — according to apologist and Catholic Answers writer Karlo Broussard, "far more reliable than other ancient texts." Sir Fredric Kenyon of the British Museum and New Testament scholar Craig Blomberg affirm that the New Testament scriptures are authentic and reliable documents, substantially handing on what was written by the original authors.

The Catholic Church, also supported by sound scholarship, agrees: "Holy Mother Church has firmly and with absolute constancy held, and continues to hold, that the four Gospels …

whose historical character the Church unhesitatingly asserts, faithfully hand on what Jesus Christ, while living among men, really did and taught. … [The authors] told us the honest truth about Jesus" (*Dei Verbum*, 19). Finally, let's put together what we already know. Jesus prayed for those who would believe in him through *the word of the apostles* (see Jn 17:20). In order for that to happen, this "word" or message must be accurately recorded and preserved for all generations. And certainly, God, who first inspired the authors of the Bible, is fully able to preserve what he inspired.

With this in mind, let's look at the Gospel of John to see just a little of what Jesus thinks about spiritual truth.

For starters, Jesus declares truth to be central to his mission: "For this I was born, and for this I have come into the world, to bear witness to the truth" (Jn 18:37). This truth, Jesus tells us, is necessary to sanctify his disciples — including you and me (see Jn 17:17).

And, as we've seen, Jesus isn't just a witness to the truth; he *is* the truth, as he says: "I am … the truth" (Jn 14:6). Truth, then, is a living, eternal reality. In contrast, Jesus describes the devil as "the father of lies" who "has nothing to do with the truth" (Jn 8:44). Notice: There is no neutral ground. Saint Paul warns, if we "refuse to love the truth and so be saved," we are opening ourselves up to the deceptions of Satan (see 2 Thes 2:10). Only those who are "of the truth" — whose character and desire align with truth — hear Jesus' voice (Jn 18:37). Those who are not of the truth, on the other hand, "cannot bear to hear [his] word" (Jn 8:43).

This is only a tiny sampling of what the New Testament says about truth, but already we can see how essential it is to believe in, seek, and live the truth. Our happiness in this life and our salvation in the next are inexorably tied to our relationship with truth. So, ask yourself: Do I believe that objective spiritual truth exists? Do I love the truth? Am I seeking it? Do I desire to live according to the truth?

Can I assume you answered "yes" to all of the above? Fair warning, it's not as simple as it first seems to carry out your intention to follow truth. Within our fallen nature, there are forces that hinder our ability even to hear truth, let alone accept it. Thankfully, God is greater than those forces. Still, we need to recognize them so we can seek God's help to resist their influence in our lives as we seek to form a contemplative heart that strives for deeper union with God.

Ears to Hear

Spiritually speaking, your ears are connected to your heart. The condition of your heart determines how well you can hear truth. And your ability to hear truth directly affects your ability to cultivate a contemplative heart. Contemplation, according to one definition, is a loving, attentive gaze on truth. Therefore, it's vital that we examine our hearts and ask ourselves — and the Holy Spirit — what might be interfering with our openness to the truth.

The fact that we have a fallen nature and live in a fallen world pretty much guarantees that we will all suffer from some sort of spiritual hearing loss at one time or another. Our fears and our sins, our wounds and our misconceptions have all contributed to our felt need to protect ourselves from what might threaten us. And sometimes we believe truth is a threat. We need Jesus to heal us, to open our ears, our hearts, and our minds to the truth that will make us free.

Part of that healing involves coming to know ourselves. We each have our individual reasons for dodging the truth. With prayer and the guidance of the Holy Spirit, you can learn what yours are, and with God's grace, overcome them. Jesus said we are sanctified — made holy — "in the truth" (Jn17:17). So this process of improving our ability to hear truth is also a process of sanctification, of becoming holy.

Below you'll find five common causes of spiritual hearing loss. Each is followed by a brief description of the lies at the root of that particular disorder and the truth that can liberate you from those lies and restore your spiritual hearing. As you prayerfully review each form of spiritual deafness, ask yourself and the Lord if any of them fit your situation. Simply recognizing the problem can be the beginning of healing.

This is simply meant to help you examine yourself with the aid of the Holy Spirit.

Desires held too tightly: You've got your heart set — on getting married, on becoming a priest, on having children or not having them, on getting that perfect job. You're convinced you need this to be happy, to "be somebody." Giving it up would feel like losing your life. If you listen to truth, it may ask you to let go of your desire.

- *The lies* — Getting what I want will make me happy. The sacrifices truth might require of me will make me unhappy. Truth is no fun. God will take from me, not add to my life. God is not the source of my happiness. God can't — or won't — make me happy.
- *The truth* — Fulfillment and happiness are found in a close relationship with God. He knows me and loves me beyond what I can imagine, and he knows what will truly make me happy, even better than I do. Happiness doesn't come from being selfish, but from love. Loving God and others, and receiving their love in return, brings a deep, lasting joy. And as Saint Augustine wrote, my heart will be ever restless until it rests in God and in his will.

Fear of what God may do or require: You're afraid if you listen to truth — that is, to God — he might ask you to be a missionary in Africa, or a priest or a nun. He might tell you to break up with your boyfriend, to pray three hours a day, and to give away twenty percent of your income, or worse — give a talk to your parish's women's group! That would be too much. You're afraid of being forced to do something that you feel is not right for you and too difficult.

- *The lies* — God will force me to do something that will make me unhappy. Or he will ask me do something difficult and expect me to accomplish it with my own strength. God would never ask me to do what I love to do, because he always asks us to do things that we would rather avoid or that frighten us.
- *The truth* — God is the one who planted my deepest desires within my heart. He wants my true identity and potential to blossom more than I do. As Fr. Michael Scanlan said, "God will not send you to Africa unless he first puts Africa in your heart." God will give me a love for the work he has called me to do. And he always gives me all the graces and strength necessary to do it. God is not harsh with his children. He doesn't push; he leads — gently.

Pride that leads us to think we know better than God: You've heard the truth — at least, with your physical ears. You know many doctrines of the Church. Perhaps you've even read the *Catechism of the Catholic Church* or the documents of the Second Vatican Council. You're aware of the Church's moral teachings. But you want the "freedom" to decide for yourself which, from among all the Church's teachings, you will follow. It's difficult for you to acknowledge that the Holy Spirit is the ultimate author of the official teachings of the Church because it's easier to disagree with men than it is to argue with God. It's better for your "freedom" if truth remains a bit uncertain. After all, you're intelligent. You don't need some authority to tell you how to run your spiritual life.

Thinking that we know better — than the Church, than God — manifests itself in different ways. For example, one person may denigrate official Church teaching found in the documents of Vatican II because she thinks it's too lax, while another seeks to change the Church's most basic doctrines, like the fatherhood of God. In either case, the self is exalted above Christ and his Church, and truth is not heard.

- *The lies* — I can decide what's true, and the more intelligent I am, the better qualified I am to determine truth. Truth is relative. Each person can generate her own version of the truth. Acknowledging the authority of Christ residing in the Catholic Church and its official teaching (including Scripture) would mean losing control of my life. Authority — even legitimate authority — is a threat to my personal freedom. Submission to authority is akin to handing the reins of my life over to a power outside myself, and I can never really trust anyone other than myself.
- *The truth* — Legitimate authority sets me free to know and live the truth and be protected from the destructive effects of error and deception. God-given authority is just that: a gift from God. I will find peace and live in friendship with God only if I humbly submit to the truth revealed by Jesus Christ through his Church. This truth is food for my soul and direction for my life. It frees me from confusion and leads me to eternal happiness with God.

Prejudice that convinces us we already know it all: You were raised Catholic. Maybe you even went to a Catholic school or Catholic college. You've heard it all, been there, done that. And it hasn't made a difference in your life. You conclude there's nothing meaningful for you in Catholicism. You're going to move on to other things — maybe other Christian groups, maybe Eastern religions, or maybe you're going to seek your happiness in the world. Or perhaps the messenger is the problem. You already know this person who claims to be sharing the truth with you. He belongs to your parish. You grew up with him. What can he possibly tell you that you don't already know? Who does he think he is? (This form of hearing loss afflicted the citizens of Nazareth with regard to Jesus — see Mt 13:53–58.)

A word of warning about the lies below: Often, these thoughts are very subtle, rooting themselves in our minds before we are aware of them.

- *The lies* — My experience and powers of perception have given me all I need to make judgments about the truth, about the Catholic Faith, and about anyone who might try to tell me something about God. I've got things all figured out. That means I can listen — or not — to the word of God or to the priest's homily. And even if I do listen, I am free to dismiss it outright if it doesn't square with my opinions. I can also accurately evaluate the character and knowledge of those who speak to me about God even before they open their mouths. And, of course, my friends, family members, and acquaintances couldn't possibly teach me anything about God. So why listen?
- *The truth* — God uses the weak, the nobodies of the world to confound those who think they're some-

body (see 1 Cor 1:27), who think they know it all. He loves to use little ones, people who no one else would choose: the youngest member of the family (like King David and St. Thérèse of Lisieux) or someone who used to be a big sinner (like Saint Paul or Saint Mary Magdalene). If I want to hear truth, I must have the attitude of a disciple, one who is always seeking to learn. True discernment is important, but it's never hasty. I should never jump to unfair conclusions about others, inspired by rash judgments. Humility will give me open ears and the ability to hear what God is trying to tell me, even through unlikely people in my life.

Doubts about the goodness of God: Maybe you've been hurt by someone in the Church, perhaps a priest or other church leader. Perhaps just seeing the suffering in the world and in your own life has caused you to doubt the goodness of God. You're angry or wounded, or both. And you don't believe there are any good answers to your questions or any remedies for you in the Church. Unwittingly, you have set yourself up as God's judge and kept him at arm's length — in effect, turning away from the truth and the healing you so need. Of course, being honest with God about your doubts and pain is healthy, but when you settle there and refuse to budge, you can thwart your spiritual progress.

- *The lies* — God must be harsh and unfeeling to allow all this suffering. By the look of things, I care more than he does. I'm right to be suspicious of God, to doubt his goodness. What else can explain the mess the world is in? Either God isn't powerful or he isn't good. (More on this subject in a later chapter.)
- *The truth* — "God is love" (1 Jn 4:8), and Jesus

> warned us that suffering in union with him is part of the Christian life — a part that will result in great personal joy if I endure it with Christ. He hasn't misled us. God has a purpose in every suffering, which will work for my good if I will trust him. Jesus is always sympathetic toward my pain, my anger, and my doubts. He will be gentle with me just as he was when he invited doubting Thomas to touch his wounds, the signs of his tender, personal love. Jesus says to me what he said to Thomas: "Do not be faithless, but believing" (Jn 20:27).

Have you recognized yourself in any of these common causes of hearing loss? If so, that's a good thing. Being able to see your personal hindrances is a gift of grace pointing out where God is inviting you to grow.

The next step is to firmly reject the lies that have hindered you and to embrace the truth. This rejection of lies and acceptance of the truth is something that you will want to do repeatedly, especially if you have been believing certain lies for a long time. Each time you do this, you will become formed in the truth and increasingly free from the grip of lies.

With regard to the personal lies we've accepted about ourselves — our lovableness (or lack thereof), our identity, our calling — the Holy Spirit, our ever-present spiritual director, can help us to expose them, and to accept the truth of who we are and who we're called to be in Jesus Christ. So, take note of those areas where you are often disturbed, where you lack peace; there is probably a lie of the enemy lurking there, one you've unwittingly accepted. Exposing it to the light of truth is the beginning of freedom.

TWO SHORTCUTS

Now I'd like to share with you two shortcuts to improving your hearing. One is a quick and simple way to discern your general attitude toward truth. The other is a powerful and direct means of becoming free from the disordered attachments that can keep you from fully embracing the truth.

I call the first shortcut the litmus test. Truth personified, Jesus Christ, is a foolproof litmus test that exposes our attitude toward truth. In Scripture, we read of the many different reactions his presence provoked, and how those reactions revealed people's hearts. The repentant, humble Mary Magdalene was powerfully drawn to Jesus. The Pharisees roiled with envy and hatred toward the Lord, exposing the murder in their hearts — their interior allegiance to evil.

What is your immediate reaction to Jesus? What about to his word?

Interestingly, intelligence and reason aren't the deciding factors when it comes to how we respond to truth. What is? Our will, and what we've chosen to set our hearts on. Listen to Jesus: "If any man's will is to do his [God's] will, he shall know whether the teaching is from God" (Jn 7:17). In other words, those who have aligned their will with God's will, who want God's will above their own, can hear truth. If you want God's will more than you "want your wants" or "fear your fears," you will have "ears to hear" truth.

Our hearing improves as we surrender our desires into God's hands, and as we learn to trust God more and listen to fear less. And remember: Our ability to hear truth is essential for cultivating a contemplative heart. As Fr. Robert Altier expresses it, "The more we are conformed to the truth, the more we will love; the more we love, the more we will share in the life of God." This is the goal of the contemplative heart!

I'm guessing you passed the litmus test with flying colors. You love Jesus. You're drawn to him. That's why you read books like this one. If that's the case, you'll find our second shortcut very appealing.

The second shortcut is what I call the ultimate attachment. Fr. Altier told us that the more we are conformed to truth, the more we will love. This is absolutely true. But the reverse is also true: The more we seek to love Jesus, the more easily and readily we will accept truth. As we grow in love for the Lord, we will gradually become free from the selfish desires and persistent fears that make us spiritually hard of hearing. "Love Me! And all your defects will vanish." Servant of God Consolata Betrone records these words as being given to her by Jesus.

Fr. Dominic M. Hoffman, in his book *The Life Within,* puts it this way: "The top of the mountain is won, most of all, by looking up at him who is there to meet us. Detachment can come about almost unnoticed if we are looking upward." Even without realizing it, as you make loving Jesus the primary focus of your spiritual life, the Holy Spirit will be working in your heart, calming your fears and transforming your desires until they become one with the heart and will of God.

So, "make love your aim" (1 Cor 14:1), and set your heart on Jesus. When he becomes your ultimate attachment, the attachments that hinder your receptivity to truth will gradually fall away. And as a bonus, while you're focused on loving Jesus, all of the other virtues will be growing as well!

We have discussed ways to improve our spiritual hearing and embrace truth, the truth so necessary for a contemplative heart. Yet daily we are faced with the currents of our culture and the winds of the world that rage against that truth. What can we do to root ourselves firmly in the truth of Christ and stand strong?

Putting Down Roots

Noted speaker and evangelist Sr. Ann Shields witnessed a perplexing sight one morning after a windstorm swept through her town. Up and down a nearby street, tree after tree was uprooted and knocked over. The trees appeared to be strong and healthy, the kind that should have been able to withstand the wind. She later learned why they fell: Their roots were shallow.

Didn't Jesus teach us this very lesson in the parable of the sower and the seed? When the sower sowed the seed of God's Word, some seeds sprouted up quickly but "since [they] had no root [they] withered away" (Mk 4:6). You can hear and even believe truth, but if your spiritual roots are shallow — if your understanding is superficial, if you fail to "cultivate" the word with meditation — it can easily be uprooted.

Saint Paul was very aware of the importance of healthy spiritual roots. In his epistles, he repeatedly reinforced the message of the Gospel so that the truth would not merely pass through the minds of the disciples, but would become deeply implanted in their hearts. He exhorted them: "As therefore you received Christ Jesus the Lord, so live in him, rooted and built up in him and established in the faith, just as you were taught, abounding in thanksgiving" (Col 2:6–7).

So, what can we do to deepen our spiritual roots? We've already seen in Chapter 1 how important it is to "remember" Jesus repeatedly, even continually, and to listen to the Gospel with fresh ears, as if for the first time. Both of these spiritual exercises nourish our roots. Here are a few more spiritual practices guaranteed to extend your spiritual root system:

- Learn why you believe what you believe. Reasons are roots.
- Meditate regularly and prayerfully on Scripture and the truths of the Faith. Roots need to be nourished.
- Live the truth you believe. Ask the Lord how you can apply the message of Scripture to your life. Roots are strengthened with exercise.

To kick off your root-growing program, I'm going to offer some reasons to believe (Step 1 above) — in the Catholic Church, in the Holy Eucharist, and in the Church's teachings about Mary. These three aspects of our faith are vital to a healthy root system. Knowing and meditating upon the reasonableness of our faith will fortify your spiritual roots and help you withstand any doubts or challenges that may arise — from within or without. In addition, being solidly rooted in these truths will ensure a stable foundation for your contemplative life.

If you are already well-versed in these reasons to believe, you can practice Step 2: Meditate prayerfully on these awesome realities. Either way, your roots will be growing!

Reasonable Faith

Pope St. John Paul II, in his encyclical letter *On Faith and Reason*, wrote: "Faith and reason are like two wings on which the human spirit rises to the contemplation of truth; and God has placed in the human heart a desire to know truth — in a word, to know himself — so that, by knowing and loving God, men and women may also come to the fullness of truth about themselves."

God calls us to use our gift of reason to strengthen our faith. One way we can do this is by learning the reasons we believe what we believe. Reasons are much more than information. They bring light and clarity. They increase faith, hope, and love. And I know from experience that they can spark joy. When reason dovetails with faith, the seeker of truth can't help but rejoice!

Every Sunday when we recite the Creed, we say: "I believe in one, holy, catholic, and apostolic Church." Since the Catholic Church is the treasury and guardian of the truth of Jesus Christ — or as Scripture expresses it, "the pillar and bulwark of the truth" (1 Tm 3:15) — it's critical that we truly do believe in the Catholic Church, not as a man-made institution, but as the Body of Christ, filled with and guided by the Holy Spirit.

Reasons to believe in the Catholic Church

Both Scriptural and historical records of the early Church support the authenticity of the Catholic Church as the one Church divinely founded, guarded, and guided by Jesus Christ. Scripture reveals that Jesus promised to build his Church and that he entrusted the leadership of his Church to the apostles. He singled out Saint Peter, entrusting him with the keys of the kingdom of God (see Mt 16:19) — signifying his authority — and charging him with the overall task of tending the Lord's sheep (Jn 21:15–17).

Historical records tell us that this divinely given authority entrusted to the apostles was handed on to others who, in turn, passed it on to their successors. Saint Irenaeus, a bishop who lived in the second century, wrote: "Those who wish to observe the truth may observe the apostolic tradition manifest in every church throughout the world. We can enumerate those who were appointed bishops in the churches by the apostles, and their successors down to our day — to whom they handed over their own office and authority." This line of apostolic succession continues unbroken right to our present day. That means — and this is worth getting excited about — the Church that Jesus founded still exists! And remember, he said that "the gates of Hades shall not prevail against it" (Mt 16:18). Jesus has always, and will ever continue to defend and preserve his Church and its teachings.

As serious and heartbreaking as the scandals and sins of leadership within the Church are, even crimes and moral failures are not reasons to disbelieve in the Church. These sins do not reflect the influence and teaching of the Catholic Church. In fact, just the opposite: They are an illustration of what happens when Church teaching is ignored. If these same men had followed Church teaching, they could have become saints. In addition, we should never let someone's bad behavior, no matter how bad, rob us of the treasure Jesus has given us in and through his

Church. For our faith in the Catholic Church is not founded on human beings but on the promise of Christ and the power of the Holy Spirit.

Reasons to believe in the Real Presence of Jesus in the Holy Eucharist

Let's combine faith and reason as we thoughtfully consider what Scripture says about the institution of the Holy Eucharist. Consider: The One who spoke and "they were created" (Ps 148:5) also spoke these words: "This is my body" ... "this is my blood" (Mt 26:26, 28). And at his word, the bread and wine obeyed, becoming the living Body and Blood of Jesus Christ. Remember, the word of the Lord "is living and active" (Heb 4:12), accomplishing what it says. Jesus also commanded the apostles to "do this in remembrance of me" (Lk 22:19). Do what? What he had done: Transform bread and wine into the Body and Blood of Christ. Whatever Jesus commands, he also gives the power to do.

This power to do what Jesus did in confecting the Eucharist — that is, transforming bread and wine into the Body and Blood of Christ — was further shared by the apostles and their successors with presbyters (priests) through the "laying on of hands," a practice that was mentioned in the Scriptures (see 1 Tm 4:14) and continues today. Jesus truly lives in our local parishes! And we can know this by both faith and reason. What a gift!

Reasons to honor Mary and to accept her as our mother:

It just makes sense! Jesus honored Mary, even acquiescing to her request for a miracle when he had other plans (see Jn 2:1–11). Jesus also ensured her care as he was dying on the cross (see Jn 19:26–27), thinking of her in the midst of his agony. As a good Jewish boy — and the Son of God — he kept perfectly the commandment to honor his mother. And he is our model.

In the Old Testament, the ark of the covenant was the most

sacred furnishing in the temple, receiving great veneration and honor. The ark was a gold-covered box overshadowed by golden angels. It contained the tablets of the Ten Commandments, manna (the miraculous bread from heaven), and Aaron's high priestly rod that budded miraculously. The ark rested in the Holy of Holies, and for God's people, it was the place of encounter with the manifest presence of God. Mary is the ark of the New Covenant. She bore the living Word of God incarnate, the living bread from heaven, and the High Priest himself. If the ark of the Old Testament was reverenced so highly, how much more should the living ark of the New Covenant, Mary, be honored and revered?

Mary is the mother of Jesus Christ, which means she is mother of *all* of Jesus Christ. And we are members of the Body of Christ. Therefore, Mary is our mother. Moreover, Scripture says that she is the mother of all those who "keep the commandments of God and bear the testimony to Jesus" (Rv 12:17). Having sound reasons to believe that Mary is our mother helps us to more readily enter into a loving relationship with her. And don't we all need the healing grace that flows through the pure heart of this perfect mother? With the assurance of faith *and* reason, we can clearly hear our Lord say to us: "Behold your mother" (Jn 19:27).

How many people leave the Catholic Church every year because they don't know the reasons behind its teachings? I was one of them. I'm so grateful that the Lord brought me back to his Church. I'm convinced I could never have understood, or fully followed, my contemplative call apart from the Catholic Church. In the Catholic Church, I learned to recognize that call and found the support I need to live it.

If contemplation is an attentive, loving gaze upon truth, could there be a better spiritual home for a contemplative soul than the Catholic Church? Not only will you find here the treasury of truth and grace, but also a rich heritage of contemplative spirituality that will guide you safely on your particular contemplative journey.

And the Lord does have a particular way for each of us. Do you want to discover yours? Then, as the next chapter explores, you will need to learn to listen to the voice of God.

Make It Your Own

Ponder: Objective truth exists, and God has made sure we can know it through the Church founded by his Son. It's impossible to grow in deep union with God or even to reach heaven apart from the truth. So, ask yourself: Do I believe in objective truth? Do I long to know it and to live by it? If the answer is yes, you are beginning your contemplative path on solid footing, and if you continue to seek truth, the Lord will fulfill your desire. If you're not convinced that objective truth exists, take your doubts to God. Ask the Holy Spirit to enlighten you. Pray: Lord, if objective truth exists, please show me, please convince me. Pray for the grace to love truth.

Pray: Ask the Holy Spirit to reveal to you any hindrances you may have to hearing truth, and any resistances or resentments you're holding onto against God or the Catholic Church. Pray for a "right attitude" toward the truth and toward the Catholic Church. Ask for the grace to be open to accept the answers you receive.

Practice: Pick a spiritual question that bothers you. It could be an issue you don't understand or a Church teaching you have doubts or questions about. Then seek. Prayerfully read about the topic in Scripture, in the *Catechism of the Catholic Church*, and in other faithful Catholic sources. Ask the Holy Spirit to enlighten you. Never fear the truth. It will set you free (see Jn 8:32)!

Chapter 3

Listen to the Voice of God

"My sheep hear my voice."
— John 10:27

Communication is the lifeblood of relationship. Everyone knows that. We hear it all the time. But what about our communication with God? How do we keep the lifeblood of our most important relationship flowing? The talking part is maybe not so difficult, but what about listening to God? Can we really hear his voice? If so, how? Those seeking a contemplative heart — a heart in constant communion with God — need to know!

The prophet Elijah, father of contemplatives, endured the shaking of earth, the stirring of wind, and a raging fire before he finally heard the "still small voice" of God (see 1 Kgs 19:12). Mary Magdalene endured her sister Martha's displeasure because she was determined to catch every word that fell from the lips of Jesus.* At the Last Supper, St. John the Beloved leaned his ear close to the Heart of Jesus, listening to more than words.

Do you share this longing to draw close to Jesus and listen? Do you sometimes wonder if you can really hear the living God speak to *you?* Let me assure you: You can. If you belong to Jesus, if you have his Spirit dwelling in you, you can hear God. Jesus promised, "My sheep hear my voice," and when he speaks to you, he calls you by name (see Jn 10:27) — individually, personally. If you still doubt your ability to hear God, consider this: The word of God commands us to "listen to his voice" (Ps 95:7). If we can't hear him, why listen?

All right, so if it is true that we can hear God, how do we hear him? Is it a booming voice from on high? Not likely, though not impossible. Still, God isn't limited to speaking audibly. He's proficient in many languages. Haven't you found that God has many ways to communicate with you? He knows what will catch your ear. He speaks to you in ways that are attuned to your personality and identity. A line in a song may move you, or maybe you receive new insight in quiet moments before the Blessed Sacrament. He may speak to you through the written word, or simply by a sense of his presence that tells you everything is going to be all right. He knows how best to reach you — he knows your language. However he speaks, we will hear him ever more clearly if we take the time to learn to listen.

To help you tune your ear to the voice of God, we're going

---

* Throughout this book, I will present the view of the Western Fathers that the sister of Martha and the woman who anointed Jesus' feet in the house of Simon the Pharisee are also Mary Magdalene. For those who would like a more thorough explanation of this view, I recommend Fr. Sean Davidson's beautiful book, *Saint Mary Magdalene: Prophetess of Eucharistic Love.* Although the Church has taken no definite position on the issue, according to Father Davidson, the view that the woman in the three accounts is one and the same "was more or less unanimously accepted" in the Western Church until the early twentieth century. Saints such as Augustine, Pope St. Gregory the Great, St. John Fisher, and St. Thomas More endorsed the position of there being only one woman as opposed to three, as have respected theologians such as Fr. Andre Feuillet, who was often quoted by Pope Benedict XVI.

to look at four of God's most frequently spoken "languages." Becoming familiar with them will help you recognize when God is speaking to you.

God speaks:

1. Through his living word
2. Through your life
3. In your heart
4. In silence

While the Bible also shows how dreams and visions are valid ways God speaks to his children, I will not explore those in this book, because I believe they are less common. Since this is a book about how each one of us can form a contemplative heart, I want to focus on the ordinary ways in which God speaks to us (if we can ever call God speaking to us "ordinary").

Jesus loves to meet us in our everyday activities, whether it's in our prayer time, during the hours of our work, or in time spent with family. He's there, and he uses small happenings to communicate with us. Becoming more sensitive to how he speaks in these little ways is part of learning to understand the "languages" of God, and vital to learning to see — and hear — God in everything. For he delights to reveal himself even in our most mundane moments. People sometimes believe that being a contemplative means having extraordinary spiritual experiences. In fact, what makes a contemplative is a growing desire and love for God that is developed in a faithful life of prayer combined with a humble life of obedience. No visions required!

So have confidence! God will help you to hear him. He wants to talk to you even more than you want from hear him.

Language One: The Word of God

God's word is more than printed letters on a page. God's Word is the second Person of the Blessed Trinity, Jesus himself, who is the Word made flesh. But God uses human words to reveal the Word Incarnate. Through divinely inspired words and teachings passed on in the Church — both in writing (the Bible) and orally, through the teaching of the apostles (Sacred Tradition; see 2 Thes 2:15) — we come to know the One who is the Word. Since both Scripture and Tradition flow "from the same divine wellspring" (CCC 80), they both "must be accepted and honored with equal sentiments of devotion and reverence" (CCC 82).

Remember that God's written word isn't like any other book. It's alive — "living and active" (Heb 4:12), breathing with the breath of the Holy Spirit, who is right there with you, *in* you, as you read. And the Holy Spirit wants to give you more than general instructions. He wants to apply the word personally to your life. To impart comfort and light, wisdom and strength, even correction — just what you need, when you need it. And when you receive God's word with faith, you can be confident that it's "at work in you" (1 Thes 2:13) even after you've stopped reading it.

To help you hear God's personal word for you through his living word, I'd like to share few practical tips:

- Come to God's word with the humble attitude of wanting to be taught, and with the intention of putting into practice what you learn. This is what it means to truly *listen* to God's word, as opposed to merely reading words on a page that we promptly forget.
- Commit to reading at least a small passage of Scripture every day. The Holy Spirit can do great things with the little we give him. Maybe you only have a few minutes during your lunch break. That's enough

time to read a paragraph or even a few lines. Make your daily habit of reading Scripture doable, something you can incorporate into your routine fairly easily. As you're able, you may want to increase the time you give to God's word. To begin, you can choose a book from the New Testament and read it through, a little each day. I suggest starting with one of the smaller books. Or you can use a resource like *Magnificat* magazine, which has daily Scripture readings, including the daily Mass readings. The Liturgy of the Hours as found in the one-volume work called *Christian Prayer* also offers an orderly presentation of Scripture, both from the Old and New Testaments. All these resources can bring you into regular contact with God's word.

- Pray before you read. Ask God to speak to you, to show you how the passage applies to your life. Notice what strikes you in the passage, whether it's a phrase or an idea. God could be speaking right there.
- If you don't have time to meditate on what you've read right then, think of it off and on throughout the day, pondering it in your heart like Mother Mary. It will be transforming you and imparting God's light to your mind, even if you don't realize it at the time.
- Another way to listen to God in his word is to ask him questions. Bring him a burden that's on your heart and ask him to give you an enlightening word. If your issue is in a certain area, look up the topic online or in a concordance and read Scriptures that relate to that specific area. Again, pray and meditate. If you let God's word sink in, something will stand out.
- Consider keeping a spiritual journal. Write down verses that especially move you during your reading.

> If you're touched by something particular, that could be God talking to you. You can also write out some of your prayers. You might be surprised at how God speaks through this sharing, and how issues become clearer. You'll remember his answers better, too.

If you get into a habit of reading a bit of Scripture each day, at least two things will happen: You will be giving God a daily opportunity to speak to you, and you will be "stockpiling" a storehouse of Scripture in your own heart, which the Holy Spirit can draw upon to give you a timely word of encouragement or instruction.

Once when I was feeling down because of some physical symptoms I was experiencing, into my mind popped this Scripture verse: "This slight momentary affliction is preparing for us an eternal weight of glory" (2 Cor 4:17). Because this word was already in my "storehouse," the Holy Spirit could bring it out just when I needed it. That's God speaking!

When you believe you've heard from God, most especially on important matters, it's wise to seek confirmation. You can do this first of all by comparing what you believe you've heard with his word. He will never say something to you that's contrary to what he's already said in his word and through his Church. Then, check the fruits of the Holy Spirit. Are you experiencing greater love, joy, peace, patience, kindness, goodness, faithfulness, gentleness, or self-control? These are good signs. If you have a spiritual director or a trusted spiritual friend, you might want to run it by them also — again, especially if it relates to important matters.

The more you hear God through his word, the more you will want to read and meditate upon it. But God doesn't just speak through his word. He also speaks through you!

Language Two: Your Life

God speaks through your life. In fact, you yourself are a "word" from God. Your physical makeup, your likes and dislikes, strengths and weaknesses, even your circumstances — everything about you has been designed with your heavenly Father's loving purpose in mind.

You have a one-of-a-kind identity and unrepeatable mission woven into your spiritual DNA and gifted to you by God. Your particular God-given mission fits who you are perfectly. Bl. Marie-Eugene of the Child Jesus taught that "a vocation [a call from God] is a harmony between being and life, pre-established in the divine plan." You will fulfill your identity, experience your greatest happiness, and make the greatest contribution to God's kingdom and the world — even if nobody notices — by finding and following the will of God *for you.*

Not only has God created *you* in a purposeful manner, but every bit of his creation is intentionally made and perpetually sustained, guided, and acted upon by our sovereign God. This reality is called "divine providence." The *Catechism* tells us, "The solicitude of divine providence is *concrete* and *immediate*; God cares for all, from the least thing to the great events of the world and its history" (303).

This truth is the basis for believing that God can speak to us, not only through creation (see Rom 1:20), but also through the events of our lives. We may not understand everything he's saying to us through these events, but, as Fr. Wilfrid Stinissen writes in his book *Into Your Hands, Father*, "The essential thing is to know *that* God means something with *all* that happens and to live in such openness and wakefulness that he can give us insight into the meaning when he wills." In other words, we must be listening for his voice in everything that happens to us.

To get you started listening to your life, let me suggest a few areas where God might be speaking:

- **Your past:** God is eternal, so your past is present to him. And he may want to speak to you about it. Dutch evangelist Corrie ten Boom believed that if you have persistent memories, scenes from the past that stand out in your mind, God has something to say to you about them. Maybe he wants to tell you about a future calling, or an old wound that needs healing.
- **People:** God uses people to speak to you in many ways. For example, to give you counsel; to provide opportunities to practice mercy; to open doors for you; even to bring out the worst in you! (Really. That's how the grime rises to the top so you can bring it to God for cleansing.)
- **Your duties:** The duties of your state in life — what your calling calls you to do — speak to you moment by moment. Here is God's will. These daily duties are his "word" to you, and your path to holiness.
- **Circumstances:** Doors are closed or opened. The weather interferes with your plans. Your health curtails your activities. You get a new boss. In all these things, which are ordered or allowed by God, God speaks. But it's important to pray, to seek *him* and what he might be saying through them. Happenings need to be discerned, taken to God in prayer.
- **Your senses:** Some people encounter God through beauty. And as Fr. Michael Scanlan noted in his excellent book *What Does God Want?,* others will "hear" him in a homily or in music, while still others "see" God's word for them in Scripture or spiritual reading. Sometimes you might even encounter God in novels or drama — movies, television, plays, or you may sense God's presence in the "smells and bells" of worship, or the fragrances of nature.

Before moving on, take a moment to consider whether God has been speaking to you in one or more of these ways. We sometimes think when God speaks, it's always something immediately positive and uplifting, but the Lord is our Healer, and that means he sometimes brings to the surface old wounds or difficult memories that need his healing intervention. Don't be afraid of this. An old hurt may suddenly rise up in your heart, or a resentment disturb your mind. That could be the Holy Spirit inspiring you to bring that wound or anger to the Lord. Talk to him about it.

You may need to do this over a period of time, but it's worth the deep healing and freedom the Holy Spirit can effect within you. Before she could fully live her Carmelite vocation, Saint Thérèse had to be healed of her tendency to be over-sensitive, which may have stemmed from experiencing the death of her mother when she was only four years old.

Another beautiful way God speaks to us, related to what we've just been saying about inner healing, is through the vitally important language of the heart. God who dwells in your heart will speak to you from *within*.

Language Three: Your Heart

God dwells within you, provided you are in a state of grace. Therefore, he can certainly speak to you from within — through words and impressions, thoughts and dreams, and also through the inner movements of your heart. These interior movements — consolation, desolation, upset, peace, confusion, joy — and their accompanying thoughts stir within each of us perpetually. But do you ever think about your thoughts? Do you notice your feelings? Or are you more often just blindly reacting to the impulses they ignite?

The good news is that you can learn to read the language of your heart and to discern what thoughts and feelings are inspired by God, which come from yourself, and which are the suggestions of the enemy. (Here, the word *enemy* refers to all that draws us away from God, including the devil, the world that is at odds with God, and the impulses of our fallen nature.) When you learn to read this language, you come to know which paths to pursue and which to reject, which thoughts are true, and which are lies from the enemy. What an aid to helping you find and follow God's will, and to hearing his voice daily!

St. Ignatius of Loyola, master teacher of discernment, has given us "Rules," or guidelines, to help us understand the language of our hearts. In fact, he wrote two sets of rules for the discernment of spirits. In this book, I can only offer highlights of these rules, but if you want to go deeper, I highly recommend Fr. Timothy M. Gallagher's books on this subject. Here we'll touch on a few of Saint Ignatius's key principles of discernment, which will give us a basic vocabulary, so to speak, of this invaluable language.

Before we begin, a warning: Be careful not to use these principles as a tool you can wield on your own. Only by the power of the Holy Spirit are they fruitful. Always acknowledge the need for the active presence of God in the discernment process by turning to him and asking for the light to understand the movements of your heart and the grace to respond in accordance with his will.

The following guidelines apply to all who seek to go forward, "rising from good to better," as Saint Ignatius expresses it, in their relationship with God. The two main types of movements that we are seeking to discern within our hearts are called *consolations* and *desolations*.

Consolations include things like peace, light, clarity, joy, an increase in faith, hope, and love. Consolations point out the way God is leading us. For example, if you experience great peace after making a decision, that peace is a confirmation that you're moving in the right direction, especially if it's a peace that lasts, not just a momentary comfort. This is a sound spiritual guideline that will apply most of the time. As a general rule, we should welcome consolations as coming from God.

However, we should have an awareness that there can be times when consolations need to be discerned more carefully. In those who have a great desire to live for God, the enemy may try to use this desire to draw them away from God's will, not by discouraging them through desolation, but by getting them enthused about another good project that would divert them from the true good that Jesus intends. So when you're trying to decide between two apparently good courses of action, consider that you may need to discern the consolations you feel toward each option to learn which are of God and which may be a diversion of the enemy.

For example, if you've already discerned a call to a particular job, and then you begin to experience consolation when you think of leaving the job and going on a mission trip, these consolations need to be carefully discerned. Take some time to pray and consider whether this new direction is God's will for you before blindly following the new consolations. Rule of thumb: Just because something is a good thing in general doesn't mean it is God's will for you. He has specific works for you to do that he "prepared beforehand, that [you] should walk in them" (Eph 2:10). Fr. Gallagher's book *Spiritual Consolation* is an excellent guide that can help you navigate this type of discernment.

Desolation includes things like disturbance, disquiet, agitations, and temptations. These are *always* from the enemy, *never* from God. Still, God can allow us to experience desolations when he sees that we will grow through the process of discerning and rejecting them. Since desolation is always from the enemy, the thoughts that come from desolation are always lies. A downward movement of the heart often "inspires" thoughts that are false — lies of the enemy. At other times, the false thoughts come first, resulting in disturbance in the heart. Either way, it's worth repeating: The thoughts that come from desolation are *always lies*. So, for example, when you're feeling down and the thought comes to you that you're worthless, you can be sure that's a lie. Refuse to accept thoughts that come with disturbance. As a rule, desolation can be, and should always be, rejected. And our Lord will always give us the grace to resist desolation and to replace the enemy's lies with the truth that comes from God.

With God and prayer, you are stronger than the enemy, so be quick and firm in resisting him. "Submit yourselves therefore to God. Resist the devil and he will flee from you" (Jas 4:7). If possible, share your concerns with a trusted spiritual advisor. Bringing burdens to light helps to lighten burdens.

As mentioned, these guidelines for discernment apply to those who are rising from good to better in their relationship with the Lord. For those heading away from God, the Holy Spirit and the enemy will work differently. The Holy Spirit will disturb the soul in order to get the person to examine his life and return to God, while the enemy will try to "console" the person, making him comfortable in his sin.

Saint Ignatius's *Examen* prayer teaches us how to practically apply these principles of discernment in daily life. Through practice, we can learn how to "listen" to the movements of our hearts and the thoughts that accompany them, and to respond by accepting what is of God and rejecting what is of the enemy. This is a daily method of making progress in the spiritual life.

The Examen prayer consists of five steps, which I will briefly list here. For a more complete explanation, I again recommend a book by Fr. Timothy Gallagher: *The Examen Prayer*.

To pray the *Examen*, follow these five steps:

1. **Gratitude:** With gratitude, review God's gifts this day. This step helps us to become aware of God's care and active presence throughout the day. We become strengthened in the knowledge that he is truly always with us. (I like to ask for the grace to remember and recognize these gifts.)
2. **Petition:** Ask for the grace and insight to see how God has been active in your life this day. The *Examen* prayer is not introspection, a self-examination that we do by ourselves. It is something we do with God, and we cannot do without him. So ask for the help of the Holy Spirit to make your prayer fruitful. He will not refuse your request.
3. **Review:** Review your interior movements — consolations, desolations — and their accompanying thoughts. This step serves to make us more aware of our thoughts and the spiritual movements in our heart, along with the effect they are having upon us. With this insight, we can better see how to follow the lead of the Holy Spirit and reject the lies of the enemy.
4. **Forgiveness:** Ask forgiveness for any faults and sins. Seeking and offering forgiveness sets us free and opens the way for the Holy Spirit to move in and through our lives. It also defeats the plans of the enemy, who uses unforgiveness to separate us from God and one another.
5. **Review:** Finally, let what you learn inform your decisions going forward. With the help of the *Examen* prayer, each day we can begin again. We can make a fresh start using the light we have been given by the Holy Spirit in this prayer.

Besides the movements in your heart, God can speak to you interiorly in other ways. For example, through a gift of the Holy Spirit, he may impart a word of wisdom, through which something becomes clear. He may also speak through your deepest desires and persistent longings. Perhaps you have an idea that just won't leave you. Interestingly, legendary orchestra leader Glenn Miller had an idea for a "sound" that he unsuccessfully pursued for years. That is, until one day, after rearranging a musical arrangement, he heard it! The unconventional idea of making a clarinet the lead of the saxophone section of his orchestra launched Miller's unique "sound" and uplifted a nation through the dark days of World War II. If you're young enough never to have heard Miller's sound, listen to *Moonlight Serenade.*

If you persevere in seeking God's will for your life, you will hear your "sound" too, and make the unique contribution that only you can make.

Two interior ways God has consistently spoken to me over the years are through a burning warmth in my heart — like when I first read the words "there are contemplatives in the world" — and through the gift of restlessness in my Christian journey, which told me, "You're not home yet; keep searching." Avery Cardinal Dulles said that a vocation or call from God is a spirit of restlessness that comes to peace when it finds the place where it can be poured out. For me, that peace came when I "discovered" the Catholic Church, and later, contemplative spirituality. In that peace, I heard the voice of God.

And that leads to another wordless language God often uses to speak to us: silence.

Language Four: Silence

Silence is truly the language of lovers, and in relation to God, it's "spoken" in contemplative prayer. "Contemplative prayer is *silence* … 'silent love.' … In this silence … the Father speaks to us his incarnate Word … the Spirit of adoption enables us to share in the prayer of Jesus" (CCC 2717). When we listen in contemplative prayer — in silence — we are seeking not so much the words of God as living contact with the Word of God, our Beloved.

Fr. Jean de Caussade explains this particular God-language:

> It is certain there is a language of the heart which God alone understands, in which we speak to Him by our desires only and other interior movements. … This language is what is called the prayer of the heart, all interior and purely spiritual. The Holy Spirit … in the depths of the soul … listens to her, speaks to her, instructs her, moves her … and shapes her to his taste. These are operations of Spirit on spirit in which the subject herself understands, it seems, hardly anything, but from which she issues with certain impressions that have totally renovated her.

The soul, drawn to silently gaze upon Jesus in faith and love, is gradually transformed: "beholding the glory of the Lord, [we] are being changed into his likeness from one degree of glory to another" (2 Cor 3:18). There is real communication happening here, but it's primarily an exchange of hearts. Fr. Dominic M. Hoffman, OP, writes of this exchange in his book *The Life Within*: "The soul is communicating with God like a compass needle drawn to a pole. Its attention and its wordless love is an act of communication."

Due to the weakness of our humanity, we struggle to stay silent for very long. And God understands this. Most of us need a few words sprinkled into our silence. But even when that is the case, "words in this kind of prayer are not speeches; they are like kindling that feeds the fire of love" (CCC 2717). A line from Scripture. A short bit of spiritual reading. Simply the name of Jesus. Toss it on the fire!

In prayer, an anonymous Benedictine monk recorded what he perceived as Jesus' word to him about silence: "The purpose of any words that I speak to you is to unite you to Me in the silence of love." Jesus goes on to say that words are necessary to support our human weakness and to give us reassurance, but: "in the end, silence is the purest expression of My love for you and of your love for Me."

The purest expression. The purest communication. This purifying effect of contemplative silence will ultimately bring about union with God, the goal of every contemplative heart. So make time for silence in your prayer. Give God a chance to "speak" wordlessly, to transform you silently.

If you pursue this wonderful adventure of listening to God, in whatever "language," you'll find yourself swimming against the current of the world. And not only of the world. Many fellow believers also don't understand the value of prayer. They echo the protest flung at Mary Magdalene when, in an act of adoration, she poured out her precious ointment upon the Body of Christ: "Why this waste?" (Mt 26:8). If you spend time in quiet prayer, many may wonder, "Why don't you do something useful?"

We need to be convinced of the value of prayer, especially the value of contemplative prayer. Because to the world, contemplative prayer looks like doing nothing. To those of us who spend time in contemplative prayer, sometimes it feels like doing nothing. Is it a waste? Or are we doing the work of heaven? How can we know? This is what we will explore in the next chapter.

Make It Your Own

Ponder: You are invited to conversation with God, Father, Son, and Holy Spirit. He wants to talk to you — and listen to you —

much more than you want to talk to him. If you give him the opportunity, he will teach you how to hear him. His words are life! They are food and strength, light and direction. They bring healing intimacy with the One who loves you as if he had only you to love.

Pray: Pray for the grace to *want* to listen to Jesus, and for the strength to take the time to do so. Ask him to help you listen with what Saint Benedict calls "the ear of your heart." Ask him to give you "an open ear" (Ps 40:6), attentive and obedient. Remember that God himself urges us, "Incline your ear, and come to me; hear, that your soul may live" (Is 55:3).

Practice: Review the four God-languages we covered. To which do you feel particularly drawn? Make a plan and determine a time when you will try to listen to God using that "language." You may find it helpful to write what you believe he's saying to you. Be patient with yourself, and with God. Remember, we grow in discerning God's voice "by practice" (Heb 5:14).

Chapter 4

Know the Value of Prayer

"Now when Jesus was at Bethany ... a woman came up to him with an alabaster jar of very expensive ointment, and she poured it on his head, as he sat at table. But when the disciples saw it, they were indignant, saying, 'Why this waste?'"
— Matthew 26:6–8

A contemplative heart is a heart of prayer, a holy meeting place for God and man. It is another Bethany where Jesus can feel at home. For this reason, keeping the flame of prayer burning within us is one of the main occupations of a contemplative heart.

But it's not easy. The Church teaches that "prayer is a battle" (CCC 2725). Even making time for prayer is a battle. We're pushed and pulled in every other direction by forces from within and without. It seems there's always a reason to let prayer go, to shorten it or do it "later" — that elusive time that rarely comes.

Of course, we know the devil would rather have us do anything but pray. (What does that tell you about the value of prayer?) But, St. Ignatius of Loyola taught, God has given us the power to successfully resist Satan, as we saw in Chapter 3. The devil's only power is our wavering will. If we're firm in our commitment to prayer, he can't stop us.

But, too often, we're not firm. Why? Does this sound familiar? You want a deep prayer life but don't know how to justify taking time away from other tasks. You feel called to contemplative spirituality, but you have twinges of guilt because you wonder whether giving yourself to prayer is selfish — or at least not as useful as doing good works.

Our cultural atmosphere encourages us to take pride in getting things done, and to make sure other people know about the things we do. This is in complete contrast to the hidden life of prayer. We're inundated with the world's messages that urge us to follow the money, promote ourselves, multiply "friends," and stay busy. A prayer life can easily wither under the barrage of such weighty and misguided demands.

More tempting to those of us who love God is the pull to participate in other good things — evangelistic projects, teaching, spreading the word of God through multiple social media platforms. (Remember what we said about the danger of misleading consolations.)

It's not that you can't engage in any of these things and be a contemplative. You can. But you have to be careful that they don't diminish your contemplative life and that you're not doing them because, as a contemplative, you are afraid you're not "doing enough." We want to do works inspired by the Holy Spirit, not by guilt or simply because they're easier than praying!

Whatever the source of the temptations, if you're going to resist the raging currents trying to push you off the path of prayer, you must be convinced of the real power and eternal value of prayer. Unless you're convinced that the work of prayer enriches the Church and elevates the world no less than active works, you'll be tempted to let it drop in favor of doing something more "productive."

Thankfully, in the spiritual heritage of the Catholic Church, there is abundant evidence of the inestimable worth of prayer. Considering this rich tradition can encourage you to make time for prayer and provide you with a powerfully persuasive answer to those who might ask: "Why don't you do something useful? Why this waste?"

Can I Get a Witness?

One of the first ways the Lord confirmed for me the value of prayer was through the testimony of trustworthy witnesses. I had a longing for prayer, even a desire to be a friend of God, but, just as I described in the last section, I wasn't sure how to justify it or whether it was truly serving anyone but myself. It was Saint Thérèse's autobiography, *The Story of a Soul*, that first helped me identify my longings for prayer and my desire to console Jesus as part of a contemplative call. Through Thérèse, I gained a new appreciation of prayer, especially contemplative prayer. Although I admit, I wondered how a call to contemplative prayer could be lived in the world.

Then, in her beautiful book *My Beloved,* I encountered the words of Mother Catherine Thomas: "There are contemplatives in the world," not just in monasteries. Those words set my heart on fire and comforted my soul. Even in the world, I could live a contemplative call to prayer. And my prayer, just like the prayer of nuns and monks, could contribute to building the kingdom of God.

The witness of both of these wonderful women taught me that prayer is a saving stream of grace that flows from the heart of God to the world — through you and me. Only God knows the full extent of its power. But for all of us, myself included, Jesus himself is the preeminent witness, both by his example and his instruction. Repeatedly in the Gospels he exhorts us to pray, urging us to ask, seek, and knock, with perseverance.

His personal example of prayer also speaks volumes, as we read in Scripture of his habit of withdrawing to pray, despite the pressing need of the crowds. If Jesus needed to pray, how much more do we? We haven't learned well enough, I think, the lesson that apart from him we "can do nothing" (Jn 15:5). If we had, we would "pray constantly" (1 Thes 5:17).

And then there's Jesus' strong defense of the contemplative Mary Magdalene. Jesus stood up for her each time she was unjustly judged. Simon the Pharisee treated her repentant tears with contempt. Martha tried to make Mary feel guilty for listening to Jesus rather than helping her. Even the apostles — most vehemently Judas — accused Mary of wasting on Jesus what could have been used for the poor. Wasting on Jesus!

Each time, Jesus rushed to Mary's defense. To Simon, he said, "You gave me no water for my feet, but she has wet my feet with her tears" (Lk 7:44). To Martha: "Mary has chosen the good portion, which shall not be taken away from her" (Lk 10:42). To Judas: "Let her alone" (Jn 12:7). And to the disciples: "She has done a beautiful thing to me.... Wherever this gospel is preached in the whole world, what she has done will be told in memory of her" (Mt 26:10, 13). How Jesus treasured Mary's contemplative heart!

I pray we will come to treasure prayer like Jesus, and be as undaunted in pursuing it as Mary Magdalene.

Jesus' witness to the value of prayer should be enough for us, but sadly, it often isn't. Certainly, it wasn't for me. I needed more, and graciously, God gave it. What follows is a small sampling of testimonies to the power of prayer. These and others I've read over the years have fortified my faith in prayer and supported it when, at times, the answers I sought were slow in coming. Haven't we all been there? Our Lord has been good to me in bringing such witnesses into my life throughout my spiritual journey, as if to say, "Never forget the treasure of prayer. Never forget your contemplative call." Each time I come across another witness to prayer, my joy in contemplative spirituality is renewed. Although I have listed just a few, I believe they are powerful enough to impart to you a confidence in the supreme worth of prayer.

As you read these testimonies to prayer, consider how you presently view prayer, and how these witnesses might deepen your appreciation of the great gift God has given us in prayer.

- St. Teresa of Ávila wrote: "All of us spend our time in prayer for those who defend the Church, … [we] stay close to the Master in silent adoration, asking him to render your word more fruitful … [We ask that our prayer] might increase the Catholic faith and procure conversions of non-Catholics; and … give the Church holy, learned, and zealous priests." Teresa staked her life that it would.
- Marta, a young Swedish Carmelite, whose story is shared in the moving documentary *The Nun*, desires to help all those who suffer around the world. She knows she can't do this physically, but she believes that by giving her life to prayer, "God is free to act as he wishes" in all these difficult situations. Through prayer, her reach becomes "limitless." Reflect on this for a moment. Through prayer, *you* can touch the world — today!
- Mother Catherine Thomas, a Carmelite nun, learned a similar lesson: "My many years in Carmel's solitude

have taught me one does not have to be physically present to ease the burdens of an anguished world."

- St. John of the Cross declared that "disinterested love for God, love freely given to God in prayer is of the greatest benefit to the Church and what she needs most." What the Church needs most! An incredible statement.
- Fr. Jacques Philippe of the Community of the Beatitudes writes: "Prayer is … an act of love for our neighbors. … [T]he mere fact of turning toward God, approaching him in faith and love, means that all the people we carry in our hearts, and even those who without our knowing it, are linked to us by a thousand invisible but real threads of the Communion of Saints, are also 'automatically' brought closer to God and benefit from it."
- Carthusian monk Dom Augustin Guillerand overflows in praise of prayer. Through prayer, he says, "enemies are put to flight. … the sick are healed, the lame walk, and the dead are raised to life. Hardened sinners are touched by grace, while the minds of men are elevated. … Divine Love comes so near to souls that He seems almost to consume them and to transform them into His own likeness."
- In her diary, *Divine Mercy in My Soul*, St. Faustina Kowalska insists, "There is no soul which is not bound to pray, for every single grace comes to the soul through prayer."
- The official teaching of the Catholic Church, as found in the *Catechism*, provides a clear and profound witness to the value of prayer in general and contemplative prayer in particular, which the Church calls "a communion of love bearing Life for the multitude"

(2719). (I recommend reading the entire section on Contemplative Prayer in the *Catechism* — sections 2709–2719. You will be encouraged to keep praying.)

Maybe the most compelling testimony comes from the hostile witnesses, who often targeted contemplative monasteries, houses of prayer, when trying to eradicate faith from society. What does the devil know that we don't? It would seem these contemplative "do-nothings" can't possibly be a threat to his realm, yet clearly, they are. That's why the Carmelite nuns of Compiegne suffered systematic persecution from the leaders of the French Revolution, who not only disbanded their monastery but couldn't even tolerate their existence when they lived apart in private homes.

But the devil's plan backfired, for these holy women sang on the way to the guillotine, offering their lives to end the Reign of Terror. Shortly after their offering was received, the terror ceased. It had been vanquished by prayer and sacrifice.

This pattern of evil targeting the Catholic Church and, specifically, its monasteries — houses of prayer with seemingly no earthly power — has been repeated throughout history. The reign of Henry VIII in England saw the widespread persecution of the Catholic Church, including the dissolution of monasteries between 1536 and 1541. In Mexico during the 1920s, President Plutarco Elías Calles enforced extensive closures of Catholic monasteries. Similarly, the atheistic government of the Soviet Union confiscated monasteries for their own purposes.

These hostile witnesses, despite their desire to crush prayer out of existence, have instead revealed the unfathomable worth and power of prayer to reach the world, to touch hearts, and to overthrow evil. But how does this work? And can those of us who do not live in monasteries participate in this great work of prayer? How can you touch souls and change the world from your living room?

Prayer's Power

The actions of one person affect, on some level, the whole of society, whether for good or ill. When we choose sin (even if our sins appear to be "private" or "personal"), families fall apart, neighborhoods deteriorate, and souls may even be lost. Thankfully, the opposite is also true. Our individual choices can spark conversion, healing, and peace in the world around us.

How much more does this reality apply to those of us who are "in Christ"? Think of it. Through baptism, we're incorporated into Jesus' Body. We become "members one of another" (Eph 4:25), forming, as Saint Faustina described it in her diary, "one organism in Jesus." This reality is referred to as the doctrine of the Mystical Body of Christ. In and through the Holy Spirit, each of us becomes part of this one Body, and like cells in a human body, there is an exchange of life flowing from one to the other.

When you sin, the whole Body suffers. But when you grow in holiness, the whole Body is elevated. This unity, founded in the Holy Spirit, isn't limited by time or space. Prayer will take you wherever you need to go.

But what of those who aren't members of the Body of Christ? Can your prayer affect them? Yes. Your prayers win for them the influence and availability of the mercy and grace of Jesus. Our Lord wants to move in their lives, but he won't violate their will. Our prayers give him, in a sense, permission to act. They can also push back the forces of darkness, allowing the person prayed for to "see the light." Through your prayers, blocked ears can be opened, hard hearts softened.

But what gives prayer its power? Sometimes it feels like we're just saying words. Yet there is more to prayer than we perceive.

True prayer both flows from and generates divine love — the greatest force in existence. This is "the love of Christ which surpasses knowledge" (Eph 3:19). In prayer, we come into contact with God and receive his transforming love, the very love that we return to him and enlist for others. This is especially true of contemplative prayer, which the *Catechism* describes as "the prayer of the child of God … who agrees to welcome the love by which he is loved and who wants to respond to it by loving even more" (2712). Although contemplative prayer is always an encounter with love, we may not always experience it as "warm feelings." Fr. Thomas Dubay teaches that contemplative prayer is a "divinely given general, non-conceptual loving awareness of God. Sometimes it is a delightful attention. At other times it is a dry desire, or even an occasion of strong thirsting for God. … [It is] 'a naked intent toward God for his own sake.'"

Regardless of our subjective experience of contemplative prayer, whether we are aware of it or not, Carmelite Mother Catherine Thomas affirms that "supernatural love is the principal effect of contemplation." And so powerful is this love that Fr. Jacques Philippe tells us in his book *Time for God* that Saint Thérèse believed "the greatest service she could render the Church … was to keep ablaze in herself the fire of this love. … And that love is practiced above all through mental prayer."

What a liberating reality! When you love God in prayer, you can be sure that you're giving to God and to others the highest possible service. This is how Thérèse, who never left the monastery and seemingly did nothing remarkable during her short life, became the co-patron of missions in the Church. Like Thérèse, you can become a secret missionary.

To remain faithful to your call to prayer, not only must you understand its value, you also need to know and embrace your part in the Mystical Body of Christ (see 1 Cor 12). This is especially true if you are called to contemplative spirituality, because it can sometimes feel to you, and look to others, like you're doing nothing. If you don't know who you are in Christ, you can easily be moved to leave prayer in favor of "getting things done." This is why even those called to active vocations (both in religious and lay life) should diligently guard their prayer life, without neglecting their active duties.

If God has given you the desire for a contemplative heart, we can safely assume you're called to contemplative spirituality in some form. What, then, is your "part" in the Body of Christ?

Know Your Part

St. Thérèse of Lisieux, you might be surprised to know, struggled with this very question of her place in the Body of Christ, and the answer God gave her is an answer for every contemplative soul.

Thérèse looked to Scripture to find her part in the Body of Christ. Reading about the different functions within the Body — the apostle, prophet, teacher, worker of miracles, administrator, speaker of tongues (see 1 Cor 12:12–31), she longed to fulfill all of them so as to give Jesus the totality of her love. Yet none seemed to describe her particular niche in the Church, until she came upon a sentence that changed her life: "I will show you a still more excellent way" (1 Cor 12:31). The way she discovered was "more excellent" than being a teacher, a healer, or a miracle-worker. "More excellent" even than being an apostle!

What was this way? It was the way of love. If we have great gifts of faith, if we can do wonders, if we give all we have to the poor, "but have not love, [we are] nothing" (1 Cor 13:2). Therefore, Saint Paul tells us, "Make love your aim" (1 Cor 14:1). Love is what makes all service worthwhile. Without it, our works are dust. Meditating upon these truths, Saint Thérèse came to understand her identity in Christ. She found her part. She was called to "be love" in the Church. (In the chapters that remain, we will be exploring what it means to live out that love in our daily lives.)

Thérèse rejoiced, as she wrote in her autobiography: "The Church must have a heart … on fire with love. I saw that it was love alone that moved [all] the other members. I saw that all vocations are summed up in love, [that love embraces] every time and place because it is eternal." Thus she discovered her place in the Body of Christ: "In the heart of the Church, my Mother, I will be love."

Why does Saint Thérèse's vocational discovery matter to us? Because the call to be love in the heart of the Church is the call of every contemplative. In the Body of Christ, contemplatives, including those of us who do not live in monasteries, are identified with *the heart*: the heart of Christ, on fire with divine love.

The heart is unseen and quiet. Its work is continuous and vital. Nothing in the body can function without the steady beating of the heart. And yet, all the exterior activities of the body are done by other parts. Similarly, contemplatives, through their union with Christ in prayer, act as the heart pumping divine, life-giving love throughout the Body. Activated by their prayer, this love flows to the Body's farthest extremities, empowering the extension of the kingdom of God.

A cinematic illustration of this phenomenon is found in the film version of C. S. Lewis's Narnian tale *Prince Caspian*. Lucy, the youngest of four siblings and definitely the contemplative of the group, flees the battlefield when it is clear the Narnians are facing imminent defeat by the Telmarines. Does she run because she is afraid or lazy? No. She flees to Aslan, the Christ figure in the story. And it is her meeting with Aslan (her prayer), though unobserved by those on the battlefield, that turns the tide, for it summons the power of the great Lion to fight on behalf of the Narnians.

But what if Lucy had tried to engage directly in the battle, taking up a sword and going out to fight? She would have looked very brave, yes. But she would have accomplished worse than nothing. This is even more true in the spiritual battle that rages around and within us. We must guard our prayer, because that is where the heart and the power of the Church reside.

Contemplative souls may have other parts to play in the Body of Christ, along with prayer, and it is vital that we discern these other functions as well, functions that the Lord has created us uniquely to fulfill. If we do not prayerfully discern our specific role in Christ's Body, we could end up trying to do works that are meant for others and failing to do the ones God intends for us. As Saint Paul writes, each member of the body must perform its own particular function. If a spiritual "ear" tries to be a "hand," it will end up frustrated and ineffective. And a spiritual "nose" should never be recruited to carry the weight of a "foot"!

The Holy Spirit will help you discern all the nuances of your place in the Body of Christ. Ask him to teach you. Knowing your part will free you from both envy (wanting the spiritual gifts that others have) and false guilt (feeling like you're not doing enough).

Jesus taught this lesson to Servant of God Sister Consolata Betrone: "You see, Consolata, in heaven every choir of angels attends to the fulfillment of its own office without envying or desiring the office of another. Thus … each one must attend to her own mission without envying or longing for something which pertains to another soul."

As a contemplative soul who makes prayer a priority, you should never envy those who are called to give more time to active works. Each of us has our call. And to be called to contemplative prayer is a great gift. For contemplative prayer is more than just the power behind good works — wonderful as that is. Contemplative prayer itself, apart from any good work, is eternally valuable.

In his book *The Secret of the Saints*, spiritual writer Chris John-Terry explains, "Contemplation is not ordered to action as a *means* to an end, but as an eminent cause to an inferior effect. Contemplation is not [merely] the means to a fruitful apostolate. It is rather the first cause and end to apostolic activity. One does not contemplate to preach or to work. Rather, one preaches and works to bring others to contemplation!"

All this pressure to prove that contemplation is not a "waste," that it supports action (and it does), while the greater truth is that contemplation is in itself the most valuable "end" we can seek. It needs no justification because love needs no justification.

This is the love that lives in heaven. This is the love that makes saints — the proper aim of every contemplative soul.

And it is only through our contact with God in prayer that we receive this divine love. Whatever other roles we may have in the Body of Christ, whether we're called to be a mother or a teacher, a web designer or a truck driver, it's this divine love born from prayer that turns our work into the work of God and turns us into saints, contagious with the transforming love of Christ. What might that look like?

Transformers

We've learned that we can affect the Church and the world through prayer, and that contemplation is valuable in itself, for itself. But there's even more. Do you know that you can transform lives just by *being* who you are?

Let me tell you a story. Corrie ten Boom, a Dutch evangelist who survived a Nazi concentration camp, entered a contemplative phase in her life after having a serious stroke. The Lord prepared her by telling her that she would soon be living closed in with him. Her union with Jesus brought her such joy that one day, though she spoke very little, she was heard to utter one word: *"Blij"* — a Dutch word for *joy.*

A troubled young man was taken to see Corrie in hopes that she could help him. What could she possibly do for him? Though Corrie was physically helpless, when the young man entered her room, he felt himself so mightily enveloped in the love of God that his life was transformed. He says of the encounter: "When I met her, such a love came from her that I immediately stopped the wrong things I was getting into."

This is the power of *being* holy. Recall that Saint Thérèse, upon the discovery of her vocation, didn't say, "I *will* love." She said, "I will *be* love." Your personal sanctification is the most powerful intercession you can offer, because it makes your soul one with our almighty Lord, Jesus Christ. Jesus, then, acts in and through you as he wills.

Philosopher Peter Kreeft insists that the way souls will be brought to Christ is by the very existence of saints. This is because, says Kreeft, the cause of the terrible state of the world is twofold: demons and sin. And of the two, sin is the more frightening:

> There is one nightmare more horrifying than being chased and caught and tortured by the Devil. That is the nightmare of becoming a devil. … What is the horror within your soul? Sin … sin means inviting the Devil in. … And that is why the Church is weak and the world is dying: because we are not saints. The weapon that will win the war and defeat our enemy … is saints.

Scripture supports Dr. Kreeft's claim that saints are God's difference-makers. Remember how God promised Abraham that he would spare the corrupt cities of Sodom and Gomorrah if he could find ten just men within their walls (see Gn 18:22)? All they had to "do" was *be* just. The potency of sanctity is such that a few good people can reverse a raging current of sin.

And sanctity is possible even for the likes of us, because nothing is impossible for God. In a eureka moment, Servant of God Consolata Betrone exclaimed: "Divine Omnipotence! I came to understand that in spite of all my utter failures and needs, God could still make a saint out of me." Hasn't he promised to "sanctify you wholly" (1 Thes 5:23)? Isn't it his will from "before the foundation of the world, that we should be holy and blameless" (Eph 1:4)?

Listen to Fr. Jean D'Elbee, a French priest who wrote beautifully about the spirituality of Saint Thérèse in his book *I Believe in Love*: "God looks much more at what we are than at what we do, and *we are, in his eyes, what we sincerely want to be for him*" (emphasis added). That's hope!

A Benedictine monk records Jesus' words to him: "The way to holiness is the path of My friendship. There are many who complicate the way to holiness who make it seem forbidding and unattainable. … Let me love you as a friend. That is enough."

This is what it means to have a contemplative heart: friendship with Jesus.

Contemplative souls in the world can share in the charisms and spiritual gifts of contemplatives in religious orders in ways that are appropriate to their state in life. It's easy to see how we can share in the charism of prayer, but what about the call to live a hidden life? Isn't a monastery required for that? How is it possible to live a hidden life in the world? We will explore that question in the next chapter.

Make It Your Own

Ponder: Ask yourself: Do I see prayer as a task to check off my "to do" list or as a "date" with the One who knows me best and loves me most? Do I realize that Jesus loves to be with me in prayer? Do I know I *need* prayer, or do I treat it as optional? What practical arrangements are needed in my life to make a regular daily prayer time possible?

Pray: Ask Jesus to give you a love for prayer and an appreciation of the value of your own prayer life. Ask that you may experience prayer as "the source of true happiness," as Fr. Jacques Philippe expresses it.

Practice**:** Spend a few minutes less each day on social media, and a few minutes more taking in the truth of God that will renew your mind (see Rom 12:2) — Scripture, Catholic books, faithful websites, etc. Commit to spending at least ten minutes a day in quiet, asking Jesus to teach you to pray. Don't give up! He will answer.

Chapter 5

Love the Hidden Life

"Is not this Jesus, the son of Joseph, whose father and mother we know?"
— John 6:42

How do contemplative religious imitate the hidden life of Jesus? Jesus spent the first thirty years of his life living in quiet and obscurity in Nazareth, and religious contemplatives follow his example in a profound way. Are they able to do this simply because they live in enclosure behind the walls of a monastery? That seems like the easy answer, but if that's what makes their life hidden, then contemplatives in the world can't possibly share in the charism of Jesus' hidden life. At best, contemplatives in the world would be sort of second-class contemplatives.

When this question came to my mind, I wanted more clarity. I decided to ask the Lord: Is contemplative life in the world, because it isn't lived in a monastery, somehow less than contemplative religious life? (Jesus doesn't mind our questions. In fact, I think he likes them.)

No sooner had I inwardly voiced my question when, very unexpectedly, I received a clear reply, which I believe came from Mother Mary: *This is more like my life*. And with her words came light: Mary, the mother and model of all contemplative hearts, didn't live her life in a monastery but in a home in a small village. The structure of her daily life really was more like mine, and probably yours, than that of a cloistered religious community.

This realization encouraged me and helped me to understand that contemplative life can be lived *fully*, even in the world. It is different from the contemplative life of those who live in monasteries, and who give up so much for love of God and for us. Yet if it's the life Mary of Nazareth lived, surely it can't be a second-class contemplative life.

As if in confirmation, I remembered what was written in Sr. Briege McKenna's book *Miracles Do Happen*: "These [monastery] walls are only physical and this is not what makes a contemplative. What makes a contemplative is enclosure of the heart." Similarly, St. Teresa of Ávila taught that the contemplative journey takes place in the "interior castle," our soul, where Jesus dwells. St. Catherine of Siena also stressed the importance of going into the inner "cell" of our being where we learn to know God and ourselves.

While physical walls can provide the quiet and seclusion that aids prayer, I'm sure even those who live in monasteries would agree that the essence of a contemplative life exists in the heart of each contemplative where she abides with Jesus.

So just how can we live in the "enclosure of the heart"? How can we live a hidden life in the world? These are good questions, and the answer is surprisingly simple: We can do so by living like Jesus, Mary, and Joseph.

Hidden in Plain Sight

What stands out about the lives of Jesus, Mary, and Joseph is that they don't stand out. Just look at the reaction of Jesus' fellow Nazarenes when he began to reveal his wisdom and power. With astonishment and indignation, they jabbed: "Where did this man get this wisdom and these mighty works? Is not this the carpenter's son? Is not his mother called Mary?" (Mt 13:54–55). In other words, "Who does he think he is? He's no better than us!"

Fr. Jean D'Elbee comments: "We must conclude from this [reaction] that for thirty years Jesus did not make a single gesture, did not say a single word which could have revealed who he was. ... He was the carpenter, the son of Joseph, and that was all."

That was all! The Son of God appeared to be just the guy down the road who builds tables. And his mother, the Immaculate Conception, appeared to be just another housewife.

How were Jesus, Mary, and Joseph hidden? *In plain sight.* Says Catholic convert Jacques Maritain: "The best way to hide anything is to make it common, to place it among the most ordinary objects." Isn't that right where you live?

You might call this "the Nazareth form" of living the hidden life, as opposed to the monastic form. St. Charles de Foucauld was one who sought to live this Nazareth life in the world. Saint Charles was a French soldier who became a Trappist brother and, later, a priest. Hungering for the life of Nazareth, he left the monastery, eventually settling in Algeria where he served the Tuareg people in the desert of Algeria. After his death in 1916, several religious congregations seeking to follow his charism were founded, including the Little Brothers of Jesus.

Fr. René Voillaume, one such follower of Saint Charles' spirituality, considered the Nazareth form of the hidden life even more hidden than monastic life. How can this be?

Voillaume explains it in his book *Seeds in the Desert: Like Jesus of Nazareth*:

> The Christ … the Incarnate Word buried himself as it were in the obscurity of the daily life of Jesus, son of Joseph. Nor was it by isolating himself that the Christ remained concealed in Jesus. To have retired from the world and gone into solitude would have been to do something abnormal which would have attracted the attention of his fellow citizens. On the contrary, he hid his higher personality by mixing with his fellow citizens, by losing himself in their midst.

Fr. Jean D'Elbee concurs: "[In the monastery] there is still the austerity of the religious habit, of the enclosure. At Nazareth there was none of this. In our time Jesus also wants hidden souls … who distinguish themselves in nothing exteriorly, but who burn interiorly."

Do you feel the call to be one of these souls? One who appears ordinary, but interiorly burns with the fire of God? I know I do. Yet this whole topic of the hidden life raises the question: Why hide? Aren't we supposed to let our light shine?

Hide and Shine

It's confusing, right? There's so much to do — souls to be saved, the poor to be cared for — and we're *hiding*? Really? Why would we do that?

Well, most importantly, because Jesus did it. Each of us is called to "reprise" some part of the life of Christ, to be an extension of his life in our time. Part of the contemplative call is to incarnate the hidden life of Jesus.

Jesus came to save the world, yet he chose to remain hidden, to refrain from preaching or healing, for thirty years. That's ninety percent of his life! Why? As Carmelite Marie-Eugene of the Child Jesus writes, "Because He judges that the most important role he has to fulfill is that of an ordinary, hidden life, which will leave him free for the primary duty of prayer." Even though Jesus had been entrusted with the greatest mission conceivable, *prayer came first.*

The obscurity of Nazareth not only provided time for Jesus' prayer, but it also became a treasury for his inner life, a "hiding place of holy joy." God, it seems, likes to guard his treasures by secreting them in insignificance. Our Lord knew better than to throw the "pearls" of his inner life before those who had no desire for them and no capacity to appreciate them. "The unspiritual man does not receive the gifts of the Spirit of God" (1 Cor 2:14). Jesus reveals himself to those who love him, just as we do.

But the hidden life is not just about hiding. Listen to Father D'Elbee: "What fruitfulness there is in self-effacement, intimate prayer, immolation, silence!" Yes, there is *fruitfulness* in this hidden life that only God can see.

The desire for this hidden life is a gift. Fr. Donald Haggerty calls this longing "a contemplative impulse": "Intense love for a God who conceals himself provokes a longing for a life of obscurity alone with him." God draws you into hiding with him. Yet, paradoxically, the deeper you go into hiding with God, the brighter his light shines through you.

Jesus explained this to Saint Faustina: "The more perfect a soul is, the stronger and more far-reaching is the light shed by it. It can be hidden and unknown, even to those closest to it, and yet its holiness is reflected in souls even to the most distant extremities of the world." That's power. That's fruitfulness. That's the hidden life.

But be aware: Something will inevitably happen to you if you live this life hidden with God.

What will happen? Inevitably, you'll find yourself living on two planes at once. Think of Mary. Outwardly, she went about her day as a lower middle-class housewife. Inwardly, her life was brimming with God's dynamism. Mary is proof that, as Wilfrid

Stinissen writes, "a life that from the outside looks monotonous and dull can be very adventurous and exciting." Saint Joseph, too, lived this "double life," appearing, as he did, to be a simple laborer. Who would ever have guessed that Joseph lived in daily loving communion with the mother of God and with the incarnate Son of God, redeemer of the world?

Father Voillaume explains this phenomenon of living on two planes: "Every man is naturally 'present' to this visible world ... the Christian, and, in a special way, the contemplative, must also be 'present' to invisible reality. ... [He] must be more present to the things invisible as they are more 'real.'" As a Christian, as a contemplative, you have within you a whole world, a whole life, which is not perceptible to others.

You share this with the saints, as Fr. Donald Haggerty explains:

> Despite all that was recounted of them, the great truth of the saints was hidden from public view ... a secret ultimately incommunicable. ... The essential truth of who they were remained enclosed in the silence of their private exchanges with God. Every saint was a contemplative, in other words, carrying on a secret, intensifying exchange of self-giving with God. We never see the fullness of this from the outside.

Like Jesus, those who belong to him are mysteries to the world. "The reason why the world does not know us is that it did not know him" (1 Jn 3:1). And yet, Saint Thérèse tells us there's glory in this mysterious life — a hidden glory.

Hidden Glory

All around us people are seeking glory from one another (see Jn 5:44). They try to garner it through the big promotion. The expensive trip. The money they've got, and the money they've spent. The people they know and those who know them. It's the way of the world, and we're all tempted to follow it. We want people to know just who we are — or who we want them to think we are.

Now look at Jesus, Mary, and Joseph in Nazareth. Nazareth was a nothing town. Mary and Joseph had just one child, who seemed unremarkable to outsiders. Joseph did manual labor. He received no big promotions. Mary took care of her family and did housework in a modest home. The only trips were probably those made for religious feasts and perhaps a family visit. Not much material for Facebook or the family Christmas letter here.

By divine design, the Holy Family's life and work held nothing, humanly speaking, to boast about. Were these unremarkable circumstances simply a disguise, a way for Jesus to lie low until it was time for him to begin his mission? Or were he and Mary and Joseph carrying on a vibrant mission even while sweeping floors and hammering nails?

Saint Faustina seems to believe they were engaged in a great — if secret — mission. In her *Diary*, she asked Jesus to "grant the grace of conversion to as many souls as the [number of] stitches that I will make today with this crochet hook." She then coaxed him to grant her request by reminding him that he saved souls through his small daily duties: "You know, Jesus, that for thirty years you were saving souls by just this kind of work."

Jesus acquiesced to Saint Faustina's request, apparently acknowledging her claim that he too saved souls by means of little tasks.

If Jesus in his hidden life was carrying out a great mission, what does that mean for us? Could *our* ordinary tasks also be filled with undreamed-of glory? How would your vision of your life change if you knew you could save souls while cleaning the sink? For one thing, you would be seeing life like the saints did.

It might sound like the crazy dream of someone who has read too many biographies of saints (in the eyes of the world, sainthood *is* crazy!), but each one of us is called to this new vision of life — and to become saints. And it is possible. Not in our own strength, but by the power and grace of God, we too can carry out a great mission in our hidden lives, doing, as Saint Paul exhorts, "all to the glory of God" (1 Cor 10:31). Scripture tells us that even our words can "impart grace" to others (see Eph 4:29).

In addition to the hidden life of Jesus, Mary, and Joseph, we have the example of saints and other holy men and women who also witness to the fact that our apparently unremarkable lives and meager efforts can carry and convey the saving power of God. There are many examples among priests and religious, but to show that this everyday way of holiness is open to even laypeople, I'd like to share with you just a few lay men and women who lived it well. All of those mentioned below, with the exception of Louis and Zélie Martin, died in the twentieth century.

Blessed Carlos Rodriguez Santiago of Puerto Rico grew in holiness while working as a clerk at a university. Speaking of Elijah's encounter with God through a "still small voice," as recorded in the Old Testament (see 1 Kgs 19:12), Carlos writes: "You must understand it is in the simple soft breeze, not in the spectacular that our Lord is to be found" (see *Faces of Holiness* by Ann Ball). That is, in quiet, ordinary ways.

Saint Pier Giorgio Frassati was a student who seemed, even to his family, not unlike other students. But quietly through his life of prayer and his love for the poor, he became a saint. His hidden holiness was exposed when throngs of the poor and others whom he had helped flooded the streets to accompany his funeral procession.

Venerable Carla Ronci, who died in 1970 at the age of thirty-four, became holy by living an interior life with Jesus in the midst of her family, friends, and parish activities. As recorded in

Faces of Holiness by Ann Ball, Carla writes: "God is in me. I am a living tabernacle. It does not have to be difficult to live in union with God. That means to live an interior life."

The parents of St. Thérèse — Louis, a watchmaker, and Zélie Martin, a lacemaker — became saints by making all the daily efforts involved in earning a living and raising their children while keeping God at the center of it all. With surrender, trust, and perseverance, they carried on through the sorrows of the deaths of four of their children, and the joys born of their happy marriage, their remaining children, and their shared love for God.

Through her writings about the "little way," their daughter Saint Thérèse helps us to understand how we can live this hidden, very ordinary way of holiness. In her own life, her path to sanctity was so hidden that most of her religious sisters believed she had done nothing in her life worth noting. (After her death, she was not only canonized as a saint, but she also became co-patron of missions and a Doctor of the Church — that is, a teacher to be especially heeded.)

Thérèse knew that she herself was nothing and her tasks of no great consequence — like us. But she was convinced that Jesus would accept even her smallest offerings and infuse them with his power. Placing them "in your divine hands will invest them," said Thérèse in her autobiography, "with infinite value." Infinite value!

As with prayer, the "secret ingredient" that makes our little works effective for God is divine love. Only this love can transform the base metal of our daily tasks into spiritual gold.

Mother Mary Francis, a Poor Clare nun, explains in her book *A Right to Be Merry*: "Mere activity in itself is quite meaningless in the eyes of God; but the meanest task done out of love for him bursts in glory on his vision. Perhaps the silent Sister cook taking fat brown loaves out of the oven … is tipping the scales of the world in its own favor and in God's." Imagine!

Huge implications flow from this truth. We learn, first, no work (unless it is sinful) is demeaning. And we do not have to strive to climb to success in our work. In fact, the door to true success is very low, requiring humility and faith more than academic degrees and connections. No one task is intrinsically more valuable than another. As Mother Mary Francis writes: "The young nun writing books or painting canvases in oils may perhaps be doing something far less important than is the old child in the infirmary patching undertunics." A leader who rules a country for selfish ambition is doing worse than nothing, but a husband who makes his wife a snack for love is healing the world.

This is the unsuspected glory of the hidden life, "the glory that comes from the only God" (Jn 5:44) and lasts forever, the glory of "Christ in you" (Col 1:27). It is the glory of divine love, the love that is the very life of your soul. Glory is not, as the world portrays it, gaining great personal honor or power. Glory is love, the love that is divine, the love that is God (see 1 Jn 4:8). By the power of this love, daily "nothings" are transformed into eternal treasures. Without it, all that we do, no matter how great it appears, is "nothing" (1 Cor 13:2).

Love, then, is everything. So, what can you do to stir into flame the divine fire of love within you?

Hidden Fire

Always remember, this fire of love is a Person. Each time you receive the sacraments, you encounter him and draw love from the one who is Love. Your personal prayer and times of Eucharistic adoration are also beautiful ways to feed the fire of divine love in your soul.

But a contemplative heart wants more than moments of encounter with the Lord, as valuable as these are. A contemplative wants to fill all of life with God. Is it possible? Yes.

Ignatian discernment, which we discussed in Chapter 3, is one spiritual practice that teaches us how to find God throughout the day, but there are others. I'd like to share with you five interior dispositions and practices that can help you live more continually and more consciously in loving contact with God.

Let's start with what's most important.

- **Believe in God's love:** Saint Thérèse tells us: "It is trust and nothing but trust that must lead us to love." The best way to grow in love is to *believe* in God's love for *you*. In fact, the spiritual director of Servant of God Consolata Betrone, Fr. Lorenzo Sales, taught that "the first requisite for practicing this life of love is to believe in Love." Our love is a response to his love for us: "In this is love, not that we loved God but that he loved us" (1 Jn 4:10) — even "while we were yet sinners" (Rom 5:8)! (Take a moment to take that in.)

  In his book *Time for God,* Fr. Jacques Philippe strongly affirms that: "Our first act of love, one that must remain the basis for every act of love is ... to believe that he [God] loves us and let ourselves be loved ... just as we are."

  Don't we usually get it backwards? We think we have to love God perfectly before he'll love us. No. As Jesus revealed to a Benedictine monk, "Perfection is the fruit of friendship with Me, not a precondition." To believe in God's love for you is an act of love for him. His love for us is so passionate and faithful that he is painfully wounded when we doubt it and comforted when we trust it. God delights in you. Believe it!
- **Treasure God's will:** In God's will, you'll find his grace and his presence, your destiny and your peace

— even in trials, which he promises to work for your good (see Rom 8:28). God's will is a concrete expression of his love for you. No matter how insignificant the event or the duty is, because it is God's will, it carries and communicates divine power. Saying "yes" to God's will opens the way for him to move in your life. And it is one of the highest expressions of love you can offer him. For, as Fr. Jean D'Elbee writes, "Love is the uniting of [your] will to God's." Here is a way to grow in love and live in contact with God at every moment of every day.

- **Purify your motives:** "I know," said Saint Thérèse, "that the fire of love is more purifying than that of purgatory." Love God, and you will purify your motives. And vice versa. Seek to do all "not in the way of eye-service, as men-pleasers, but as servants of Christ, doing the will of God from the heart" (Eph 6:6), and your love will intensify. And as your inner "eye" becomes focused on God, your heart will become free. Check your heart by asking yourself: What am I seeking? Whom am I trying to please?
- **Guard your peace:** St. Francis de Sales urges us, "Because love only resides in peace, always be careful to conserve … holy tranquility of heart. … None of the thoughts that render us anxious and agitated in spirit in any way comes from God. … These are the temptations of the enemy."

  The devil knows the importance of peace, so he does everything he can to agitate us. If we don't discern this tactic, we can mistakenly put all our efforts into fighting things or people who agitate us, rather than using our strength to keep our peace. But when we focus our efforts on maintaining our peace, God fights all our other battles for us. Fr. Jacques Philippe writes in *Searching for and Maintaining Peace*, "Too many people are distressed because they are not contemplatives. They do not take time to nourish their own hearts and return them to peace by gazing with love on Jesus."

In saying that we need to take time to *return* our hearts to peace, Father Philippe is implying that keeping our peace is a battle. Throughout the day, we will encounter sources of anxiety — from within and without. But as soon as we notice that we've lost our peace, we can *turn again* to Jesus, asking him to help quiet our hearts and minds. He may show us the root of our anxiety, or he may remind us of his word: "Let not your hearts be troubled" (Jn 14:1). Perhaps, simply the sense of his presence or the thought of his name — *Jesus* — may recall us to peace. (There can, of course, be levels and types of anxiety that require professional aid; yet even here, seeking peace through legitimate spiritual means, such as we're suggesting, can only aid the process of healing.)

- **Practice the presence of God:** This spiritual practice contains within it all the previous principles we've discussed. Living with an awareness of God's presence will strengthen your belief in his love, increase your desire to do his will, and deepen your peace.

  Practicing the presence of God is simply believing and remembering that God — the Father, Son, and Holy Spirit — dwells within you. Through this exercise of faith, you make real, living contact with God. Each attentive glance, each turn of the heart, each word addressed to him calls forth the flow of his

> love. As recorded in the *Carmelite Proper of the Liturgy of the Hours,* St. Gregory the Great taught, "Wherever we direct our mental gaze, there we may be said to stand. That is why Elijah said, 'The Lord lives in whose sight I stand.' He did indeed stand before God, for his heart was intent on God." And Carmelite Brother Lawrence of the Resurrection writes in his work *The Practice of the Presence of God*, "Through our continual attention to God, we will crush the head of the devil and make his weapons fall from his hands. ... This [practice of God's presence] is what the spiritual life is all about."

If you live this way, eventually, your life will become "a quiet uninterrupted conversation with God," as Pere Jacques Bunel expresses it in his book *Listen to the Silence*. In this way, God will be continually kindling the fire of love in your heart.

But can laypeople, lay contemplatives, love God as fully as priests and religious? Or does our lay state intrinsically limit our love? Can you, as a layperson, give God everything? Can you become the spouse of Christ? This is what we will reflect on in the next chapter.

Make It Your Own

Ponder: For Christians, especially contemplatives, the inner life is of primary importance. How much attention do you give to your inner life with God? Do you realize that your interior life determines the value of everything you do? Consider that by your union with Christ, your daily "nothings" can be invested with infinite power and worth. What might this look like in your daily life?

Pray: Ask Mother Mary and Saint Joseph to intercede for you, praying that you would be given a deep interior life with Jesus. Pray that you may "know the love of Christ which surpasses knowledge, that you may be filled with all the fullness of God" (Eph 3:19).

Practice: Throughout the day, live the contemplative spirit by making a conscious effort from time to time to turn your attention to the God who lives within you. Speak to Jesus. Listen to him. Enjoy his presence, remembering that at every instant he is loving you.

Chapter 6

Welcome the Bridegroom

"The two shall become one flesh. This is a great mystery, and I mean in reference to Christ and the Church."
— Ephesians 5:31–32

Mixed messages keep a relationship from moving forward. You don't know where you stand or where you're going. Clarity, on the other hand, brings harmony and progress. When the relationship in question is your relationship with God, it becomes all the more critical to gain this clarity. The mixed messages of which I speak center on the layperson's call to holiness which, of course, is a call to grow in our relationship with God.

As Catholic Christians, most of us have probably heard of the "universal call to holiness" as taught by the Second Vatican Council; that is, that every person is called by God to a life of holiness. Yet, at the same time, the laity have also heard other messages, messages that could lead us to believe we are not meant for the heights of holiness; but rather, for something less — some less demanding and less rewarding form of holiness.

Specifically, we in the laity may have heard that we do not have a call to perfection, as taught by Christ (Mt 5:48). Perhaps we have heard that because we have a family and live in the world, we aren't able to love God with an undivided heart or give ourselves totally to him. We may also have picked up on the message that if we're married, a spousal relationship with Christ is not open to us. These graces, we may have been taught, are meant for those in priestly or religious vocations.

It can be confusing. We are called to holiness, but not the fullness of holiness, not the fullness of love?

If we have accepted messages like these without question, a few things could happen. We could simply continue living with the confusion born of the mixed messages. Or, we could settle down to a mediocre life of faith, believing that's where we belong. If we have a great desire to give our lives totally to God, we might live with an undercurrent of sadness because we believe our state in life prevents us from offering God this complete gift of love. Or perhaps we decide to press forward, seeking to give our all to God but never being sure it's truly our call.

Only if we gain clarity on our call to holiness, if we learn what's meant for us as laity, can we go forward on our journey toward holiness with assurance and peace.

Certainly, as laypeople, we don't want to grasp for something that isn't meant for us, but neither do we want to fall short in responding to our Lord's call to love. Just as those in religious life are seeking to be perfect, to love God with an undivided heart, to give all, and to be a spouse of Christ, we need to see what our Lord has to say about each of these things as it applies to our particular state in life.

Practically Perfect

So let's consider whether laypeople are called to the "perfection" of holiness. We first need to know what is meant by *perfection.* It *doesn't* mean "perfectionism" or being a "perfectionist." I once heard that a perfectionist is someone who takes great pains and passes them on to others. (You probably know one or two people like this.) This is *not* Christian perfection.

When Jesus speaks of being perfect, he does so in reference to love (see Mt 5:43–48). Those who love only the people who love them, love imperfectly. Jesus calls his disciples to more. He calls them to forgive, pray for, and even love their enemies, as God loves his enemies: "You, therefore, must be perfect, as your heavenly Father is perfect" (Mt 5:48).

This seems impossible, but Saint Thérèse says Jesus can require this kind of love from us because he puts it within us. "God's love has been poured into our hearts through the Holy Spirit who has been given to us" (Rom 5:5). God gives us what he asks for. When you were baptized, you were given the three theological virtues: faith, hope, and love. That is, supernatural, divine love. We receive it in "seed" form, which we can then choose to nurture — or not.

And this *choosing* is important, because perfect love is rooted in the will. As Fr. Costanzo Antonellis wrote in his book *A Saint of Ardent Desires:* "Perfection is love of God. And the perfect love of God is the complete union of your will with God's. … The more you desire to unite your will with the Will of God, the greater will be your perfection."

This call to perfection is not a special call meant only for priests and religious. Listen to what one Reverend Mother told a young woman who said that she wanted to enter religious life to follow her "special call to perfection": "My child, the call to perfection is not a 'special call.' All Christians are given this counsel. The First Commandment is for everyone. … And it is possible for your sisters [in the world] to attain a higher degree of perfection if they love God more and serve him better than you do in the cloister."

This is the call to holiness that the Second Vatican Council famously proclaimed to be "universal" — for everyone.

Pope St. John Paul II wrote about this universal call in *Christifideles Laici*:

> Everyone in the Church, precisely because they are members, receive and thereby share in the common vocation to holiness. In the fullness of this title and on equal par with all other members of the Church, the lay faithful are called to holiness: "All the faithful of Christ of whatever rank or status are called to the fullness of Christian life and to the perfection of charity."

Notice how all are called to the fullness of holiness. No half measures. This claim is supported by God's word, which declares, "he chose us in him before the foundation of the world, that we should be holy and blameless before him" (Eph 1:4). "The God of peace" wants to "sanctify you *wholly*" (1 Thes 5:23–24). Could it be any clearer that this call is for all of us?

Wrong Division

What about the message that the layperson in the world is prevented from loving God with an undivided heart? Admittedly, loving God with our whole heart might seem very difficult, particularly for married people, who may feel like their hearts are divided, parsed out among children, the family pet, their spouse, and God (hopefully, not in that order!). Yet, as we've seen, the First Commandment says every single person is to love God "with *all* your heart" (Mt 22:37).

Some will quote Saint Paul to argue against this point, referencing his first letter to the Corinthians in which he says that a married man or woman is "divided." To understand this text fully, it's important to be precise. Saint Paul did *not* say that a married person's *heart* is divided, but that a married person's *interests* are divided. And the difference is crucial.

He writes: "I want you to be free from anxieties. The unmarried man is anxious about the affairs of the Lord, how to please the Lord; but the married man is anxious about worldly affairs, how to please his wife, and his *interests* are divided" (1 Cor 7:32–34). This passage is commonly misread to say a married person's *heart* is divided. As a result, many well-meaning people assume that a married person can't possibly give God a wholehearted love. It seems like simple math, but it is misguided.

To believe that the love you give your spouse reduces the amount of love you "have left" for God is to apply earthly principles to a heavenly subject. Love — especially divine love — isn't a finite object, like a pie that shrinks when it's shared. No. That's earthly math.

The heavenly math of love is very different. When love is shared, it doesn't diminish. It grows. If you love God, all your other loves — as long as they're in accord with his will — are enriched. When you love God, you love your spouse better. And when you love your spouse, you're loving God.

Do people in religious life love God less because they love their brothers and sisters in religion? Did Mary love God with a divided heart because she also loved Saint Joseph? The answers are obvious.

But what of this problem of divided interests? Yes, it can be difficult to focus on the Lord in the midst of varied interests, particularly the demands of family life, but I'll bet many priests and religious would say that their lives are no less demanding. Fr. Dominic M. Hoffman, OP, points out in his book *The Life Within* that even in the cloister, the problem of divided attention exists.

The solution, he says, is to grow in prayer. Habitual inner prayer will enable us to keep our inner attention on God even in the midst of activity — whatever our state in life.

The bottom line here is this: Divided interests, of themselves, can't divide hearts. Regardless of your state in life, you can determine to love God with your *whole* heart. This is the way of a contemplative. And our God deserves nothing less.

All for All

Priests and religious leave their jobs, homes, and families all for love of God. Many offer their lives by making vows — of poverty, chastity, and obedience — to God. Yet it is also true that, as the *Catechism* teaches, every disciple is called to live these evangelical counsels in accordance with her state in life (915). The difference is that religious men and women take vows to follow the evangelical counsels of poverty, chastity, and obedience "within a permanent state of life recognized by the Church" (915), thus even giving up the possibility of marriage.

Though we laypeople do not live in the same permanently vowed, officially recognized state, that does not mean we are "free" to run our own lives, to do whatever we want to do, to follow the morals of the world, and seek first the kingdom of money. That would not square with being a disciple of Christ, for all disciples are called to a life of obedience — to the Lord, to his word, to his Church, to his Spirit (see Rom 8:14). Therefore, Saint Paul reminds us, "You are not your own; you were bought with a price" (1 Cor 6:19–20). In baptism, you vowed your life to God. Every Easter season at Mass, you renew those baptismal vows.

Still, do our baptismal vows really mean that we are called to give God everything? Consider the words of Jesus: "Whoever of you does not renounce all that he has cannot be my disciple" (Lk 14:33). For "whoever would save his life will lose it, and whoever loses his life for my sake will find it" (Mt 16:25). Renouncing all means surrendering our lives to God and putting everything in his hands, to do with as he decides. This includes our very selves, as Saint Paul teaches: "Present your bodies as a living sacrifice" (Rom 12:1).

Giving your life to God doesn't necessarily require cloisters and habits. Rather, it calls for a daily surrender of your will. For, as Fr. Jacques Philippe explains, "the man who has given his will to God has, in a certain fashion, already given him everything."

Yes, priests and religious make a beautiful, noteworthy, and obvious "up-front" sacrifice of their life with the clear intention of giving themselves to God. Sadly, this isn't how many people in the world live their single lives or enter married life, though it can and should be. Every vocation calls for an offering of our lives to God, and every life involves sacrifice. Think of the sword of pain and sacrifice that pierces the heart when a spouse is ill or dies. Or when dreams must be laid down, or relationships given up. To say nothing of the sacrifices that come with children! Or, the inability to have children.

Without doubt, there are differences between priesthood and religious life, and the lay vocations of marriage and the single life. But in every vocation we are called to give our life completely to God. This is the spiritual path of a contemplative heart, for, according to Father Philippe: "We are deluding ourselves in aiming to make progress in prayer if our whole life is not marked by a deep sincere desire to give ourselves totally to God, to make our lives conform to his will as fully as possible."

Whatever your state of life may be, know that you're called to give all, in a wholehearted, perfect love of God. That sounds like spousal love, doesn't it?

Holy Matrimony

You may have wondered, especially if you're married, if you too can be a spouse of Christ. Both Scripture and Church teaching assure us that each of us is called to spousal union with Christ. Again, this is not reserved for those in priesthood or religious life, but is for all the baptized, men and women alike. And, in fact, sacramental marriage to a human spouse is not a hindrance to spousal union with Christ, but it is an aid, for those who are called to it. To understand this more fully, we must first ask: Just what is sacramental marriage? This is a huge question, but let's hit the highlights.

First, marriage is a vocation. It is a call from God. (Take that in.) Fr. Robert Altier writes in his book *God's Plan for Your Marriage:* "Marriage is first and foremost a spiritual reality." Marriage is not simply a worldly path, or "what you do when you *don't* vocation." No. Marriage is itself a full-fledged vocation. And Father Altier reminds us that "although marriage may be the most natural state of life, the call to that life and the person with whom that life is to be shared need to come from God" and, therefore, must be discerned. It is hardly a worldly path.

Too often in our parishes, group prayer for vocations focuses solely on the priesthood and religious life. The silence on the vocation of marriage speaks volumes. We're seeking the fruit of priestly and religious vocations without tending the tree from which they come: the pivotal vocation of holy marriage. As marriage goes, so goes the individual and the family, the priesthood and religious life, the Church and society as a whole.

Marriage is, secondly, a sacrament. The *Catechism* teaches that the "covenant [of marriage] between baptized persons has been raised by Christ the Lord to the dignity of a sacrament" (1601). As one of the seven sacraments, marriage is a sign and an instrument of communion with God "by which the Holy Spirit spreads the grace of Christ the head throughout the Church which is his Body" (774). For the source of sacramental marriage is divine love: "Christ the Lord abundantly blessed this many-faceted love, welling up as it does from the fountain of divine love and structured as it is on the model of His union with His Church" (*Gaudium et Spes,* 48). Marriage is all about living and nourishing our life with God. In fact, Father Altier affirms, it is "specifically designed to make spouses saints."

One young man who was drawn to marriage feared if he married, he couldn't become a saint. His professor, Blessed John Duns Scotus, assured him: "It's the only way you can be." Why? Because marriage was his particular path to holiness, chosen for him by God.

Marriage is a miracle. Spouses, says Father Altier, "love each other with the love of God that has been given to them." This is "unconditional" love … love in "the highest sense." This love of God is first given to us in the Sacrament of Baptism (CCC 1266). Then, in the Sacrament of Matrimony, God gives graces that are particularly suited to the needs of the vocation of marriage and that make it possible for spouses to share this unconditional love with each other. Only with the grace God provides in the Sacrament of Matrimony can spouses share with each other the divine love that is fundamental to their call. Marriage is truly a miracle — a work of God beyond natural human ability. Impossible for us, but for God "nothing will be impossible" (Lk 1:37).

Finally, marriage is a prophetic sign. Sacramental marriage is an image of the marital union of Christ and the Church: "A man shall … be joined to his wife, and the two shall become one flesh. This is a great mystery, and I mean in reference to Christ and the church" (Eph 5:31–32). The *Catechism* describes Christian marriage as "an efficacious sign" of "the covenant of Christ and the Church" (1617). It is, as Fr. Robert Altier describes it, "a foreshadowing of heaven, the marriage banquet of the Lamb."

Marriage is not an obstacle to union with God, but the very means he chooses to bring about such union for those who are called to this vocation. So let's be careful not to treat sacramental marriage as a worldly venture. In her commentary on the book of Tobit, Angela Carol argues that the many suitors of Sarah were struck dead "because they had not regarded marriage as holy"! We too suffer when we fail to regard marriage as holy. Families fall apart, and vocations — even souls — are lost.

Love for your husband or wife doesn't disqualify you from a spousal love for Christ. And you mustn't let it. Let me borrow the words of a wise Reverend Mother to a young postulant named Maria, who found she was falling in love with a man (Captain von Trapp, to be exact): "If you love this man, it doesn't mean you love God less" (*The Sound of Music*). For no human being, not even a human "soulmate," can fill the infinite need and longing of your soul. You *need* Jesus as your spouse. Nothing and no one can take his place.

The Church agrees: "The Apostle [Paul] speaks of the whole Church and of each of the faithful, members of his Body, as a bride 'betrothed' to Christ the Lord so as to become but one spirit with him" (CCC 796). St. Teresa Benedicta of the Cross adds, "With the most tender love will he [Jesus] seek to win every single one as a bride." He is seeking *you*. And "as the bridegroom rejoices over the bride, / so shall your God rejoice over you" (Is 62:5).

Wonderful, isn't it? But it puts us in a bit of a bind. If laypeople are called to perfection, *and* to love God with our whole heart, *and* to give ourselves completely to him, even to be his spouse, then what is it that distinguishes priesthood and religious life as "higher" states of life? Just how are they "higher"?

How High?

Let's be clear. The Church does teach that priesthood and religious life are higher states of life than the lay states. But, as we've seen, it is not a call to greater holiness that makes them "higher," for we are all called to the fullness of holiness. In fact, priests and religious are meant to be icons pointing us to that holiness, not signs telling us the road is closed. They are meant not only to be saints, but also to raise saints (see Eph 4:11–13), to "be a stimulus and a help to their brothers and sisters striving to follow Christ," as the World Synod of Bishops on Consecrated Life declared in 1994.

So again I ask: Why are priesthood and religious life called *higher* states of life?

There's a clue in the very phrase "higher states of life." Do you see it? Their *state* of life is higher than the lay state. That is, their situation, the circumstances in which they live. These circumstances are generally a great aid to living a holy life. They're pre-ordered to seeking God, with such things as prescribed times of prayer and easy access to Mass and the Blessed Sacrament.

Fr. Constanzo J. Antonellis explains: "Priesthood and religious life offer many advantages, [so that] all things being equal, [they] are the highest vocations because they more directly lead to God." These "many advantages" are what Saint Paul was referring to when he said an unmarried man can more easily keep his attention on God.

However, and this is very important, if you are called to a lay vocation in the world, the Lord has arranged that all the advantages *you* need will be found along the path of your vocation. In the very situations, people, and work to which he has called you, there you will find the graces (the advantages) you need to become holy.

In his book *Searching for and Maintaining Peace,* Father Philippe warns that it is a common temptation to believe that "in the situation which is ours (personal, family, etc.), we lack something essential and because of this, our progress, and the possibility of blooming spiritually is denied us." While objectively speaking, priesthood and religious life have greater advantages than lay vocations, when it comes to each individual person, the greatest advantages are found right in the vocation to which we are called.

There is another vital phrase in Father Antonellis's explanation: "all things being equal." All things being equal, priesthood and religious life are higher states of life. The priesthood, it's been said, is so great that we'll never fully understand it in this life. Does that mean it's always better to be a priest or religious?

Fr. Timothy Gallagher tells the story of a young man named Bruce who believed being a priest was "the best thing to do," the way he could most please God. So he tried to suppress a persistent longing for family life. Until one day, distressed and confused, he heard an inward word: "I have something else for you." He took it to be Our Lady's voice, and he says, "It set me free." Eventually, he married, and he knew great peace and certainty in his vocation.

For Bruce, priesthood wasn't the highest or best thing he could do for God. And that's because "all things" are never "equal." We're created as unique individuals, entrusted with particular missions. The best thing we can do for God is his will. And only by doing God's will for our lives can we become saints. And there's nothing higher than that!

We all know that priesthood and religious life are holy vocations. But, laments Father Altier, "All too often people think of marriage as a lesser vocation." Sadly, too many people do not realize that the lay vocations of marriage and the single life lived for God are also holy vocations. Yet we *need* to know this if we're going to follow God to the heights of holiness in the particular vocation he has prepared for us. We need to know that deep union with God — holiness — is meant for each one of us. Only then will we be awake and ready when the cry comes: "Behold, the bridegroom! Come out to meet him" (Mt 25:6).

The next two chapters will help us become ready to meet Christ our bridegroom. What we're going to look at next is an important part of our growth in holiness, one we might wish we could skip. We can't. But, in the end, we'll be glad.

Make It Your Own

***Ponder*:** Think a moment. Have you been influenced by the idea that laypeople are called to a lesser type of holiness than priests and religious? How has this affected your spiritual life? Going forward, what might you change?

***Pray*:** Ask the Lord to give you his vision of your call to holiness and the grace to live it. Ask him to transform the way you think about your spiritual life in light of what you've just read.

***Practice*:** Prayerfully read Ephesians chapter one, asking to have "the eyes of your hearts enlightened" (v. 18), to know the hope of your great call. Then … keep reading! God has more good news for you.

Chapter 7

Let Suffering Work

"For this slight momentary affliction is preparing for us an eternal weight of glory beyond all comparison."
— 2 Corinthians 4:17

When you get married, you get the whole package — the whole other person "as is." And maybe you get some surprises! The same is true of our spousal union with Jesus. When we marry Christ, sooner or later we find we have married a crucified Bridegroom — and he's inviting us to share his cross. Jesus brings the cross into our lives because he knows it provides blessings and graces that we can receive no other way. Carried with faith, the cross gradually sets us free from the world, the flesh, and the devil, and unites us with the Heart of Jesus. It leads to joy.

Along with the hidden life of prayer, sharing in Jesus' sacrifice is integral to the contemplative call. In fact, every Christian is given a share in Jesus' cross. But take heart: As you share Christ's sufferings, you will share abundantly in his comfort (see 2 Cor 1:5).

The suffering of the cross comes in many forms. In this chapter, we're going to focus primarily on physical suffering because it touches almost everyone. And because it's a form of suffering I feel somewhat "qualified" to speak on, having lived with the chronic — and potentially dangerous — disease of lupus for most of my adult life. Still, much of what we will discuss in this chapter applies to other kinds of suffering as well as physical suffering.

But you might wonder, if we're concerned with the spiritual life, why focus on physical suffering? Because suffering, especially physical suffering, can affect every aspect of our being, including our interior life. Sickness and pain can cause our spiritual life to sputter and stall, or to deepen and grow. What makes the difference is our response to it.

We know Jesus still heals. But what if he allows you to suffer rather than healing you as you hoped? How do you keep the faith and your peace in the face of continued suffering?

Follow the Healer

Miracles do happen. But if they're not happening for us, doubts, confusion, and even guilt can arise in our hearts. Our faith can be shaken, our prayer life threatened with extinction, and our questions turned into accusations.

That's why even before seeking answers to our questions about healing, it's vital to fortify our relationship with God. When we are confident in God's goodness and convinced of his personal love for us, we'll be ready to hear his answers.

To strengthen our bond with our heavenly Father, we can begin by deliberately meditating on what we *know for certain* about the love and faithfulness of God — from Scripture and Church teaching, and from our lived experience with him. Remember who he has been in your life — the times when you've experienced his presence, the ways he's touched your life. Recall prayers that *were* answered as you hoped.

Do this regularly, and especially when you feel yourself sinking. Fr. Jacques Philippe says that through our "personal experience of God re-encountered, recognized and loved in prayer — [we] *taste and see how good the Lord is* (Psalm 34)," which builds within us an "unshakable confidence."

After reminding yourself that "God is love" (1 Jn 4:8), that he can't be anything else but loving (even when we don't understand what he's doing), resolve to practice this simple principle: *Don't let what you don't know (or don't understand) cause you to lose what you do know.* Don't let your questions and doubts cause you to lose your grasp on what you know about God's goodness and his constant, tender love for you.

Your strong relationship with God is your greatest support when facing suffering. And it's the safe place from which to ask tough questions.

Disclaimer: You might not get all your questions answered. That's because both suffering and healing are mysteries. Still, a mystery isn't something we can't know anything about; it's just something we can't know *everything* about. This means we can learn something from it, and about it. So, since we can learn *something* about sickness and healing, let's briefly take on a few of the most commonly asked questions:

- **Should I ask for healing or should I accept my illness as God's will?** Ask! Go to Jesus as one who welcomes and loves you. As Sr. Briege McKenna says, "Don't you be making up Jesus' will for him." Let him decide. And always remember: "Every one who asks receives" (Mt 7:8). Prayer will always bring forth good results of some kind — grace, intimacy, new light. And yes, sometimes even healing.

- **If Jesus healed everyone in the Gospels, doesn't that mean everyone should be healed?** *Sometimes,* as in the event recorded in the eighth chapter of Matthew, Jesus "healed all who were sick" (v. 16; see also Lk 4:40), but not always. Jesus healed just one of the multitude of sick lying around the pool of Bethesda (Jn 5:8,13). And when Saint Paul begged three times to be freed from his thorn in the flesh (2 Cor 12:7), his request was denied. Instead, Jesus promised him grace and strength. Then there's Timothy, who had chronic digestive troubles (1 Tm 5:23). If you're not healed, don't fret. You're in good company. And good hands.
- **Is it my fault if I'm sick?** Although sickness came into the world through our first parents' sin, it doesn't automatically follow that sickness is caused by our individual sins. In a couple of instances, Jesus indicates that sin may have caused an illness (see Jn 5:14, Lk 5:20–25), but overwhelmingly, this is not the case. In the healing of the man born blind, Jesus explicitly states that the man's blindness was *not* caused by either his sin or his parents' (Jn 9:3). You can certainly ask if there's any hindrance to healing in your life, but if you're not shown anything specific, be at peace. Trust God's love for you. Remember, the devil is the accuser. God's correction is always gentle, loving, and clear.
- **Is it my fault if I'm not healed?** Wrong teaching in some Christian circles has led people to believe that if they are not healed, they must be doing

something wrong, like not believing enough or not praying the "right" way. This is false teaching. Your faith is in Jesus, not in your faith! You believe in him and his ability to heal you. That's enough. There's no need to work yourself up into a frenzy of "faith." That's not the attitude of a child of God secure in her Father's love.

- **Why does Jesus sometimes delay in answering our prayers?** Out of love. Consider Jesus' response when Lazarus was ill: "Jesus loved Martha and her sister and Lazarus. So … he stayed two days longer in the place where he was" (Jn 11:5–6). Why? To give them a greater miracle. Similarly, in her book *Miracles Do Happen,* Sr. Briege McKenna tells the story of a young boy diagnosed with a brain tumor. His family prayed together every day for his healing, and after two long years, the boy was healed. Why the delay? Through those days and months of prayer, God transformed the whole family — even the teenagers! Now that's a miracle.
- **Is there a time when I should stop persistent prayers for healing?** In her book *Healing: Bringing God's Gift of Mercy to the World,* Dr. Mary Healy shares some wise advice: "Pray with great confidence in the Lord's will to heal, yet leave the outcome entirely in his hands. Keep praying persistently until healing occurs, or until there is a sense that the Lord is leading you to pray in a different direction, or until the sick person has a joyful and peaceful assurance that their affliction is part of the Lord's perfect plan." As recorded in her biography, *Mother Elisabeth* by Marguerite Tjader, St. Maria Elisabeth Hesselblad asserts that such "unanswered prayer" is

a call to live "a supernatural life, a life of special dependence on [God]." And, we might assume, special closeness.

- **If Jesus can heal me, why doesn't he? What good does it do to leave me ill, especially when I could do so much more for his kingdom if I were well?** This is a question we'll be taking up in the next section. For now, I will say this much: Being sick, weak, or disabled won't disqualify you from serving mightily in the kingdom of God.

Finally, let me assure you that there's a path to healing and wholeness open to everyone — even those who aren't physically healed. Physical healing is very important, but it isn't what matters most. If your soul is whole, you're whole, even if some of your parts don't work so well.

In her book *Miracles Do Happen,* Sr. Briege McKenna relates the words of a father whose young daughter had just died: "I realize now that healing doesn't mean getting my way, but getting the strength and the grace to say yes to God's way." The essence of healing, in every situation, is saying "yes" to God. Nothing is better for you or your loved one than God's will, even when it's painful. Saying "yes" to God brings inner healing and profound peace. This is the healing that makes you ready for heaven, and makes you ready to say, like Saint Paul, "For me to live is Christ and to die is gain" (Phil 1:21).

The Paradox of Power

Seeking God's answers about sickness and suffering will challenge you to see things in a new way — God's way. We tend to think that physical infirmity, especially when it's long-term, is a waste and a hindrance to doing God's work. Of course, we need a measure of strength to do anything, but Jesus reveals that our personal strength isn't where the real power lies.

Paradoxically, real power, divine power, is found right where we find ourselves much of the time: in weakness and sufferings big and small. The very things we would like to avoid bear within them a hidden treasure: "the power of Christ" (2 Cor 12:9). Your weakness is an ideal staging ground for God's strength. That's why Saint Paul could say, "When I am weak, then I am strong" (2 Cor 12:10).

This isn't how we naturally think. We're more like Peter, who wanted to rescue Jesus from the suffering of the cross. But Jesus strongly "rebuked" Peter, saying: "You are not on the side of God, but of men" (Mt 16:23). Peter needed the Holy Spirit to transform his vision. And so do we. Imagine if Peter had kept Jesus from the cross. All would be lost — literally! And if you and I escape our cross, who might miss heaven? For through our cross, we partner with Jesus in saving souls.

How, then, can we learn to see like God? Usually through a combination of his word, pondered in prayer, and our own struggles with suffering. In an earlier chapter, I mentioned a day when I was feeling especially lousy and complained to the Lord: "What good is this?!" Immediately, the words came to mind: "an eternal weight of glory." These words from the second letter of Saint Paul to the Corinthians (4:17) helped me to see my suffering not as a waste, but as God saw it — something powerful and purposeful, something that was part of his plan for my life. I was learning to see through God's eyes.

As we've seen, Saint Paul, too, complained about his stubborn thorn in the flesh, begging Jesus three times to remove it. Instead, Jesus said: "My grace is sufficient for you, for my power is made perfect in weakness" (2 Cor 12:9a). With this new vision, Paul exclaimed: "I will all the more gladly boast of my weaknesses, that the power of Christ may rest upon me" (2 Cor 12:9b).

Your weakness, your need of whatever sort, acts as a conductor, drawing the power of the Holy Spirit into your life.

In his book *Five Loaves and Two Fish,* Venerable Francis Cardinal Van Thuan tells how he learned the lesson of God's strength in our weakness. While a prisoner in Vietnam, he came to his lowest point. Feeling helpless and useless, he prayed, pouring out his heart to God. Suddenly, he saw "as if in a vision … Christ on the cross, crucified and dying. He was completely helpless … certainly worse off than me in my prison cell. Then I heard a voice … saying: 'At this precise moment on the cross, I redeemed all the sins of the world.'"

Cardinal Van Thuan understood that his weakness could save souls, for through it, he was one with Christ on the cross. This is the holy paradox of power. "The word of the cross … is the power of God" (1 Cor 1:18)! Saint Paul tells us we are "always carrying in our bodies the death of Jesus," and it is for this very reason that "the life of Jesus may also be manifested in our bodies" (2 Cor 4:10). Our wounds may not appear in the literal form of the wounds of Christ, like the stigmata of St. Francis of Assisi or St. Padre Pio; nevertheless, we do truly bear our Lord's wounds, each in our own way. And we will share in his victory.

Now the words of Saint Paul become clearer: "In my flesh I complete what is lacking in Christ's afflictions for the sake of his body, that is, the Church" (Col 1:24). In Christ, the Head of the Body, the "afflictions" are complete. What is lacking is our participation in these sufferings. The sufferings of the Head — Jesus — must be "distributed" throughout the body (us) in order for Jesus' redeeming sacrifice to reach the world.

Suffering in itself isn't redemptive. But suffering that is joined with Christ's and offered with love — that is, with the desire and intention of serving God and helping others — becomes a powerful saving force. "If I deliver my body to be burned, but have not love, I gain nothing" (1 Cor 13:3). What a thought! Martyrdom offered without love is "nothing," but the smallest suffering (a sore toe, sand in your shoes) offered with love unleashes the redemptive power of Christ.

Allow me to echo Venerable Archbishop Fulton Sheen's famous remark: "Don't waste your suffering!"

Cross-training

Our suffering can help save the world, yes, but it can also help *us*. Our trials are an invitation to a spiritual education and a personal transformation. God is at work in them, making us — like Jesus — "perfect through suffering" (Heb 2:10). That is why Saint James says, "Count it all joy, my brethren, when you meet various trials, for … the testing of your faith produces steadfastness. And let steadfastness have its full effect, that you may be perfect and complete, lacking in nothing" (Jas 1:2–4).

Through our difficulties, Father God is growing us up, setting us free, enriching us with graces, and making us capable of experiencing spiritual joy. "[God] disciplines us for our good, that we may share his holiness. For the moment all discipline seems painful rather than pleasant; later it yields the peaceful fruit of righteousness to those who have been trained by it" (Heb 12:10–11). God wants us to "share his holiness," which is the greatest possible happiness, both in this life and the next. (Take a moment to drink that in.)

In his book *The Way of Trust and Love,* Fr. Jacques Philippe tells us that every trial carries within it a call from God, a call that seeks a response. To discern God's call in each particular trial, Father Philippe suggests we ask ourselves: "What act of faith am I being invited to make in this situation? What attitude of hope am I being called to live by? And what conversion in relation to love … am I being summoned to undertake?" Asking ourselves questions like these is a beautiful and fruitful way to face every problem.

Writing in *Contemplative Provocations,* Fr. Donald Haggerty affirms: "We need to understand the providence of God differently. Trials do not reflect a sign of disfavor with God. Rather, the reverse is indicated. God is offering us an invitation. … He is teaching us. … Everything God permits is inseparable from a very personal love he extends to us in a trial." How would your life be different if you saw your difficulties and sufferings this way? If you believed each one came from God's very personal love for you and carried with it divine gifts? If you've given your life to Christ, this is the actual truth of the matter — difficult as it may be to see at times. God *is* working in *everything* for your good (see Rom 8:28).

But a word of caution: If we refuse to see God's hand in our crosses, if we become bitter and blame God or others for our troubles, we can thwart his purposes for our lives. So let me ask you again: How would your life be different if you really believed God is working for your good in every one of your troubles? That he's got a gift for you in each trial? One thing is certain: Your burdens would be lighter.

Lighten the Load

Two very familiar commands of Jesus seem to be at odds with each other: (1) "Deny [yourself] and take up [your] cross daily and follow me" (Lk 9:23), and (2) "Take my yoke upon you. … For my yoke is easy, and my burden is light" (Mt 11:29–30). Aren't you tempted to ask, "Which is it, Jesus, a heavy cross or a light yoke?"

Maybe Jesus is saying that if we carry our cross the way he intends, the way he carried his, it will seem light (or, at least, lighter). How did Jesus carry his cross? Consider:

- He accepted his cross as coming from his loving Father: "Shall I not drink the chalice which the Father has given me?" (Jn 18:11).

- He carried all the Father gave him, but *only* what the Father gave him.
- He never forgot that he was accomplishing a great work through his cross, that his suffering was purposeful.
- He bore it willingly, out of love for us and for his Father. He gave his life; it wasn't taken from him (see Jn 10:18).
- He drew strength from his relationship with his Father and the support of Mother Mary.
- He never lost sight of "the joy that was set before him" (Heb 12:2).
- Finally, he forgave.

What about us? Don't we often resist our crosses? We blame others, circumstances, or even God for our suffering. We add to our cross weights God never intended us to carry — fear, anxiety, depression, guilt, anger, impatience, rebellion. Rather than being aware that we're doing a great work, we think of our cross as pointless. And rather than carrying our cross for love, we become fixated on ourselves. Too often, we forget God's presence with us, and our prayer grows cold. The vision of the joy set before us dims, and we walk precariously near the edge of bitterness.

What crushing weights have we have added to our cross! How much lighter would it be if we carried it the way Jesus carried his, the way he told us to carry ours? Listen carefully to his instructions: "Deny [yourself] and take up [your] cross daily and follow me" (Lk 9:23).

First, Jesus says to deny yourself. How do we deny ourselves? By deliberately choosing God's will over our own. We trust his judgment more than ours. We believe his words of love and constant care over what our feelings might be telling us. And we let God decide what he will allow and how things will turn out, trusting that his will is love. Of course, we can only do this if we are daily praying for the grace to put him first and trust him completely. We won't do this perfectly, but Jesus is interested in our desire and our smallest efforts. When we care and we are trying, he is pleased.

Next, Jesus says to take up your cross. One way to help overcome our resistance to suffering is to consciously accept — to take up — our cross, and remind ourselves that it comes from God, even if it passes through human channels. Acceptance doesn't eliminate hope for relief or change. Remember, God in his sovereignty can deliver you instantly. Two times he granted me a few hours during which I felt perfectly healthy. Those experiences taught me that I was completely in his hands and that, at least for now, this illness was his will. That knowledge has brought me great comfort.

Note also that Jesus tells us to take up our own cross, not the crosses of all the people suffering from wars, disasters, illnesses, and accidents that you hear about on the news. God gives you the grace to carry your cross, not those of others. (That doesn't mean we don't have compassion for the sufferings of others. We certainly do.) Also, don't carry imaginary crosses. Mark Twain once said he had lived through many difficulties, most of which never happened. How many imaginary sufferings have you lived through?

In addition, carry just *the cross given you by God.* Some sufferings are self-made, coming from our faults, sins, and poor decisions. A chronic complainer carries a heavy self-made cross. As we grow in maturity and holiness, such self-imposed crosses will lighten. Meanwhile, God, in his goodness, will use even our faults and sins for our benefit! They are great teaching moments.

Jesus further specifies that we are to take up our cross daily. Just carry *today's* load. Ask the Holy Spirit to forgive and heal the past. Leave it to God's mercy. Entrust the future to his faithful providence. God gives grace for today, so live in the present moment. If we choose to carry yesterday and tomorrow — for it is our choice — we will end up doing it in our own strength, and it will feel very heavy indeed!

Finally, Jesus instructs, "And follow me." Look to Jesus. Love him. And listen to his words: "Let not your hearts be troubled" (Jn 14:1). He's with you — in you — every step of the way. He's your "Simon of Cyrene," sharing your cross, gently easing your burden. In his presence, you will find strength and joy, even in suffering. Remember, he's guiding you to a happy end. For crosses always end, but joy is forever.

If you practice carrying your cross this way, I guarantee you a lighter load.

But just in case you'd like a little more help, the saints tell us of a powerful spiritual practice that engenders love, joy, and interior freedom even in the most difficult circumstances. This will be the subject of the next chapter.

Make It Your Own

Ponder: Consider how the mighty sovereignty and tender love of God use our weakness and suffering to bless us and save the world. How does God's view of suffering and sickness differ from the way you usually see things? What spiritual lessons do you think God has been teaching you through your difficulties? What act of faith, hope, or love might he be calling you to make? Does knowing that your trials serve a great, eternal purpose give you a new sense of meaning?

Pray: Ask for the grace to accept rather than resist your cross, and for the faith to trust God's plan for your life. Ask the Holy

Spirit to show you any ways you might be adding "weight" to your cross. Each day, in a short prayer, offer all your sufferings to the Father in union with Jesus' Most Holy Sacrifice being offered in every Mass throughout the world. As you go through your day, say little prayers like: "For love of you, Lord," or, "Jesus, save souls." Finally, remember to call on Mother Mary's intercession in all your difficulties. She wants to help you with everything.

***Practice*:** Take time to meditate on what God says about suffering. (Some suggestions: any of the Gospel accounts of Jesus' suffering, such as 2 Cor 4:7–18; 1 Pt 1:3–9; Col 1:24; 1 Pt 3:20–24.) Practice "returning" to the present moment when you begin to worry. Entrust both your past and future to the merciful love, power, and wisdom of God. He's got you!

And remember, in the end, "The Lord Jesus … will change [your] lowly body to be like his glorious body" (Phil 3:20–21). That's reason enough to, as Saint Paul loved to say, "rejoice in the Lord always" (Phil 4:4).

Chapter 8
Grow Through Surrender

"Father, into your hands ..."
— Luke 23:46

Surrender, relinquishment, abandonment — call it what you will, it can be a frightening prospect for all of us who so love to be in control. We see loss of control as a threat to all we hold dear, not the least of which is ourselves. This is a natural, very human way to respond. But (surprise!) it's not God's way.

Jesus tells us: "Whoever would save his life" (that is, hold it tightly to himself) "will lose it, and whoever loses his life for my sake" (that is, surrenders it to me) "will find it" (Mt 16:25). To lose your life in this context means putting it in the hands of the One who knows you best and loves you most, the one who can make you who you were created to be. He's the only one who can "find" your life for you. When you surrender, you aren't rolling the dice and hoping for the best. You are relying on a sure thing — the love of Jesus Christ. It feels risky, true, but it's the safest and sanest way to live. And it leads to the holiest and happiest outcome.

A Snapshot of Surrender

We might think surrender ought to be reserved for the spiritual thrill-seekers. But in fact, surrender is our basic Christian call. It is simply to give our lives totally to Jesus Christ. Father Joseph Schryvers, in his book *The Gift of Oneself*, explains more fully:

> To give oneself to God is to [entrust] to him one's body and one's soul, to abandon to his care all one's powers, aspirations and affections, desires and fears, hopes and plans for the future. … [It is] to deposit in the Heart of Jesus all preoccupations, all solicitude, and the thousand perplexities of daily life; it is to confide to him all one's interests, charging him to provide for everything, to make all things right.

Servant of God Luis Maria Martínez, the late archbishop of Mexico City, writes in his book *Only Jesus* that to surrender is to "live in the arms and in the heart of Jesus, and … [that] he, with incomparable solicitude, will rule over all things including each detail of [your] life, designing all for [your] good and for [your] happiness."

This surrender not only fosters happiness; it also kindles divine love.

In his book *I Believe in Love*, Fr. Jean D'Elbee shares the wisdom of Saint Thérèse as regards surrender and love: "Jesus deigned to show me the road that leads to this Divine Furnace, and this road is the surrender of a little child who sleeps without fear in its Father's arms." Surrender became Thérèse's only "compass" in the spiritual life.

Fr. Jean-Pierre de Caussade, author of the famous spiritual work *Abandonment to Divine Providence*, taught that through surrender we foster not only love, but also faith and hope. He wrote: "The state of self-abandonment is a blending of faith, hope, and love in one single act which unites us to God in all his activities." Notice how surrender simplifies the spiritual life into "one single act."

Finally, surrender brings peace — "the peace of God, which passes all understanding" (Phil 4:7). We are in right relationship with God when we surrender, and somehow our whole being knows it.

Happiness, faith, hope, love, union with God, and peace — these are the fruits of surrender. Who wouldn't want all of that? Those of us seeking a contemplative heart can hardly resist. But, let's face it, surrender is still a scary prospect. Yes, we sincerely believe in God's power, in his goodness and love. But surrender asks, "Do you believe in it enough to stake your life on it — your health, your finances, your family, your job?" It's the difference between *believing* that someone can push a wheelbarrow over Niagara Falls on a tightrope, and volunteering to *get into the wheelbarrow*.

Only God's grace can get us to the point where we trust enough to hop into God's wheelbarrow. But God will never withhold his grace from those who ask for it. Our part is to prepare ourselves to receive his grace by developing our trust in him.

How can we do this? To fully trust God, we must first be convinced that he is infinitely powerful, the sovereign ruler over all, that he really does have it all under control.

Sovereign Security

Is God absolutely sovereign over absolutely everything? If you believe God's word, it isn't difficult to answer this question. The sovereignty of God is one of the Bible's most celebrated themes. It's sung in the psalms: "The Lord has established his throne in the heavens, and his kingdom rules over all" (Ps 103:19). It's demonstrated in every book of the Old Testament where we witness God deposing and raising kings (see 1 Sm 15), giving life in "impossible" circumstances (Gn 21), and even parting the sea (Ex 14).

In the New Testament, Jesus reveals the all-encompassing power of divinity as he heals the blind, raises the dead, and commands the wind and waves with a word (see Jn 9, Jn 11, and Mk 4, respectively). He declares unequivocally: "All authority in heaven and on earth has been given to me" (Mt 28:18). At this very moment, he is seated at the right hand of the Father "far above all rule and authority and power and dominion" (Eph 1:21), accomplishing "all things according to the counsel of his will" (Eph 1:11), watching over even the fall of the sparrow and numbering every hair on your head (see Mt 10)!

Church teaching confirms: "His might is universal, for God who created everything also rules everything and can do everything. God's power is loving, for he is our Father, and mysterious, for only faith can discern it" (CCC 268). Saint Augustine affirms: "Nothing happens that the Almighty doesn't will to happen, either by permitting it or by himself doing it."

Yes, God's got it under control — all of it!

I realize this statement is both comforting and disturbing. Of course, we don't want a chaotic, random universe. But we may wonder, if God's in control, why are things such a mess? Why does he allow so much evil?

Important questions. If we're going to surrender to God, we need to know that he's not only sovereign, but good.

All Good

How many of us get stuck right here, doubting God's goodness?

Rather than humbly seeking answers from God, we add up the evidence of suffering and evil in the world — what we can see, what we think we know — and we pronounce judgment: God can't be good if he allows so much suffering. And we can become hardened in our position, pinning our rebellion on a good cause: our concern for the suffering, which we imagine is greater than God's. This attitude injects an undercurrent of distrust in our relationship with the Lord and hinders our ability to receive authentic answers to our questions.

But we don't have to get stuck here. We can begin right now to bring our questions to the Lord with a humble, teachable spirit. If we do this, what might we learn?

Well, first, we would learn that it wasn't God who brought evil and suffering into the world. Human sin did that, and we've all contributed our share. What God did, in Jesus Christ, was to take upon himself all the guilt of all the sin ever committed, or that ever will be committed, so we could be free, so we could have eternal life. He found a way — at great cost to himself— to clean up *our* mess.

But why, if he's all-powerful *and good,* doesn't he just put an end to evil and suffering? He will. That's the plan. But he wants as many people as possible to receive eternal life. So he's giving humanity time. And the freedom of choice necessary to choose salvation — which necessarily means we also have the freedom of choice to choose sin. Saint Peter, speaking of Jesus' return in glory, says, "The Lord does not delay his promise … but he is patient with you, not wishing that any should perish but that all should come to repentance" (2 Pt 3:15, NAB). He allows temporary pain only to procure eternal gain beyond all measure, for as many as possible.

"OK," you say, "but meanwhile, people are still sinning, evil is still flourishing. Why doesn't God make it impossible for us to sin, to continue to choose evil?"

Think with me for a moment. It is only possible to *choose* the good, to choose to love, if you have *a choice* — that is, if it's also possible to choose *not* to love, if it's possible to choose evil. True love must, of necessity, be freely chosen, freely given. Forced "love" is no love at all. Yes, God wants our love, but he wants real love. That means he must give us a choice and allow for the possibility that some will refuse to love, which opens the door to evil in their own lives and, as a result, in the world.

But if we've truly grasped the value of eternal love and the eternal life it imparts, we would say without hesitation that being able to love is worth the temporary suffering of enduring evil. Saint Paul said as much: "I consider that the sufferings of this present time are not worth comparing with the glory that is to be revealed to us" (Rom 8:18).

Even while we await the final destruction of evil, God doesn't just let us suffer pointlessly. He allows only those sufferings to touch our lives that he knows will serve us and form us into the saints he intends us to become. Remember, getting to heaven isn't just about getting *somewhere,* but about becoming *someone.* In this way, God turns evil and suffering on its head, causing every one of our troubles to work to our advantage, as well as for the good of others: "We know that in everything God works for good with those who love him" (Rom 8:28).

The Church reassures us of this:

> God is in no way, directly or indirectly, the cause of moral evil. He permits it, however, because he respects the freedom of his creatures, and mysteriously knows how to derive good from it: "For almighty God ... , because he is supremely good, would never allow any evil whatsoever to exist in his works if he were not so all-powerful and good as to cause good to emerge from evil itself." (CCC 311, interior quote, Saint Augustine)

Although this is always true, recognizing God's hand in everything is, for most of us, a gradual awakening. Pope Benedict XVI understood this: "God wants from us ... a down payment of trust. He says to us: 'I know you don't understand me yet. But trust me: believe me when I tell you I am good and dare to live on the basis of this trust. ... Behind the difficulties of your life, a love is hiding." (Consider that these words were written by a man who lived in Nazi Germany under the rule of Hitler.)

We learn to see this hidden love through faith and experience. Even the apostles were slow to grasp this reality. When Jesus told them he was going away, they were heartbroken. But he assured them: "It is to your advantage that I go away" (Jn 16:7). And it was. But did they believe him? Do we?

Jesus directed them to the joy that was to come. And we need to remember that too — often. How could a pregnant woman endure the trials of pregnancy if she never thought about the joy of seeing her baby? Yet we so easily forget that all our trials are contributing to an immense joy that awaits us.

As pilgrims in this world, we need to keep before our eyes the vision of the "shrine" to which we're heading — our heavenly home — and to remember always the One who walks with us. When you get to know him, to truly know his heart, you won't wonder if God is good. You'll know. Then, the troubles of life won't be able to shake your faith or discourage you from entrusting your life to Love.

It's Who You Know

To know God is eternal life: "This is eternal life, that they know you the only true God, and Jesus Christ whom you have sent" (Jn 17:3). How important it is, then, to get to know him! The alternative is to one day hear those chilling words: "I never knew you" (Mt 7:23).

In biblical terms, "knowing" means more than to be acquainted with someone. To "know" someone, according to God's word, is to have an intimate, interior, experiential knowledge of another, resulting in a communion of hearts. This is what Jesus was speaking of when he said: "I am the good shepherd; I know my own and my own know me, as the Father knows me and I know the Father" (Jn 10:14–15).

When you know God like this, you will experience his goodness and come to believe in his love. In his book *Jesus Appeals to the World,* Fr. Lorenzo Sales writes: "To believe in Love … means to believe that … everything he [God] does or permits … is always for our best. Only a few souls … possess this loving and practical faith in Love." Longing for more such souls, Jesus pleaded with Servant of God Consolata Betrone, "Do not make me out a God of rigor, whereas I am naught but a God of Love!"

Knowing Jesus will instill within you an unshakable loyalty, even in the face of suffering or "unanswered" prayers. Even when you don't understand what he's doing, you'll still trust because you know *him.* Saint Peter didn't understand any more than the other disciples Jesus' teaching about eating his body and blood. But because he knew Jesus, his trust was firm. When Jesus asked his disciples if they also wanted to leave him because of this hard teaching, it was Peter who answered: "Lord, to whom shall we go? … We have believed, and have come to know, that you are the Holy One of God" (Jn 6:68–69).

How can you get to know him like that? As with any relationship, you spend time with him. You listen to him. You share your heart with him. Over time, I guarantee you will come to know Jesus better and better. If you need something more specific as you get started, try the powerful spiritual practices below. With the Holy Spirit's guidance, you can determine how and when each practice might be used to deepen your intimacy with God.

- **Know Jesus through his word.** What would you think of someone who claimed to know you but never listened to what you said and ignored every letter, text, or email you sent? Too many Christians treat Jesus this way. And we are the ones who lose because the word of God is not just informational; it's transformational. It has the power to align our hearts and minds with the heart and mind of Christ. Says Fr. Sean Davidson: "Many of our problems [including our inability to trust God] come from incorrect thinking. … [The word of God] acts upon our minds and transforms our way of thinking, bringing deep peace to the soul as well as sanctifying our desires." Through meditation on God's word, you will "be transformed by the renewal of your mind" (Rom 12:2) until you "have the mind of Christ" (1 Cor 2:16) … until you *know* him.
- **Encounter Jesus' presence in the sacraments and in contemplation.** Without fail, you contact Jesus' living presence in the sacraments. He's present to you. Be sure to be present to him. Acknowledge his presence. Talk to him. Love him. Thank him.

  In contemplative prayer, you can also have a real, direct experience of God dwelling within your soul. There's a deep, unspoken "knowing" shared by the soul and God in contemplative prayer. Notice that it was the contemplatives — Saint John, Saint Mary Magdalene, and, of course, Our Lady — who stayed with Jesus through his suffering. And it was a contemplative once again, Mary Magdalene, whose love and loyalty for Jesus remained strong even at the tomb, when everything seemed lost. When you seek to know Jesus like this, you will become over-

> whelmingly attached to him, and your fear over what you might lose through surrender will lessen — because your Treasure is secure.

There's something else that might lessen your anxiety about surrendering. I've found when I want to do something that causes a little fear and trepidation, it helps to watch someone else "go first." Of course, Jesus is our premiere model of surrender, ever uniting his will to his Father's. But sometimes it can help to have examples from the ranks of "regular" people to help inspire us to take the leap of surrender.

You First

The call to surrender will likely come at the cutting edge of our growth, that place where the Holy Spirit is asking us to change, to take a new step, or simply to trust. Often, it's where our fears rise up and our cherished desires threaten to slip away. Our first instinct will likely be to protect ourselves, to stay where we feel comfortable and in control. These are moments of decision. And moments of grace.

The wife of the author Nathaniel Hawthorne faced such a moment when their eldest daughter, Una, suffered for four days with a high fever. The doctor warned that if the fever didn't break soon, the girl would die. Unwilling to bear the thought of losing her daughter, Mrs. Hawthorne desperately begged God to heal the girl, but there was no change.

Finally, worn out by her struggles and fears, Mrs. Hawthorne came to a decision: "I will not doubt the goodness of God." She prayed: "Lord, I give her into your hands to do with as You know best. I surrender her to Your goodness." To her amazement, the anguishing mother was now filled with peace. Not long after, the girl's fever broke, and she began to get well. When the mother laid down her will and surrendered the outcome of her daughter's illness into God's hands, he took over.

In this case, surrender led to the pray-er receiving what she desired. Sometimes, however, God works in a different way, as I've learned from personal experience.

In the early years of my marriage, I had a great desire to have children, but it wasn't happening. My desire was so strong that seeing a baby or toddler caused an almost physical pain. One morning when thinking about this, I heard inwardly, "Will you let me decide?" At that moment, I was given a grace beyond myself to say, "Yes, Lord, whatever is best for your kingdom." Then came the words: "Am I not more to you than ten sons?" (1 Sm 1:8). The validity of this experience was confirmed by its results. The painful longing was gone. In its place came a sense of contentment. And although I never had children, ever since that day, seeing babies and little ones brings delight.

Another call to surrender came many years later when tests revealed the possibility of cancer. I told the Lord, "I really don't want this." Later, while praying the first sorrowful mystery of the Rosary, the Agony in the Garden, I asked the Blessed Mother to gain for me the grace of Jesus' surrender to the Father's will. As I prayed, my dread drained away. I went through two surgeries with a steady peace (nourished by spiritual reading, particularly the *Spiritual Letters of Father P. J. de Caussade*). Thankfully, the results were good: no cancer. And I had learned firsthand the power of the Rosary and the place of Our Lady in helping us to surrender. A lesson to remember.

Just one more personal example to hopefully lift your heart. Many years ago, on my way to my college internship at a local hospital, I felt like skipping out. I'd had a rough morning. Instead, I asked the Lord to take over the whole day. That day, the man I would marry asked me out for the first time. You never know what God will do if you give him just one day!

Along with the big issues of life, surrender can also make a life-changing difference in our everyday struggles. Fr. Jean Pierre de Caussade was assigned to a position that filled him with dread. But, as he recounts in one of his *Spiritual Letters,* when he turned the whole matter over to God: "God removed from my heart all the old repugnance [and gave me] a certain peace and liberty of spirit at which I was myself astonished."

So, there you have it. Real life examples of surrender. Hopefully, watching others go first has inspired you to take your turn and entrust all to God. And, as Pope St. John Paul II famously said, "Be not afraid!" For the call to surrender is a call to victory.

The Victory of Surrender

We associate the word *surrender* with defeat. But in the spiritual life, the opposite is true. Surrender is not giving up, but giving God full access — to your heart, your problems, your gifts, your whole life. When you do, he can work with freedom, bringing to bear all his power, wisdom, and love. How could you lose?

Rather than burdening you with a multiplicity of spiritual methods, surrender offers an uncluttered path to holiness, for it "encompasses everything else" in one spiritual way. As Carmelite priest Fr. Wilfrid Stinissen writes in his book *Into Your Hands, Father*, "The one who willingly lets himself be led by God [in this way] walks a very straight path. He saves an infinite amount of time and trouble" and comes more quickly to union with God. Similarly, Father D'Elbee tells us, "This simple abandonment [surrender] is the peak of holiness, the peak of love."

The ability to surrender is ultimately a gift from God, who is actively "at work in you, both to will and to work" (Phil 2:13) this grace into your soul. That's encouraging, isn't it? But what is your part in receiving this gift?

Along with persistently asking for the grace of surrender, strive to have *goodwill.* Goodwill is the habitual disposition to prefer God's will to your own. It aligns your life with his. Goodwill is so powerful that during an exorcism performed by the saintly Fr. Jean-Joseph Surin, the demons admitted, "We are able to surmount all obstacles; there is only this bloody dog of good-will, which we have never been able to deal with!"

The opposite of goodwill is resistance to God's will, habitually preferring your own will to his. Fr. Stinissen writes that this resistance "creates an inner cramp, which is the most significant reason for people's unhappiness." Our resistance to God's will is, in essence, a resistance to our own happiness because all that God gives us, and only what God gives us, will lead to true lasting happiness. Having goodwill — that is, wanting God's will — is good for your mental health!

If you're not sure you have goodwill, ask for it. Pray: "Lord, make me willing to always choose your will over my own." Then, do your best to exercise this goodwill, always asking for divine assistance.

A practical tip for growing in trust and exercising goodwill comes from a Benedictine monk who writes that Jesus taught him to deepen his trust "by entrusting to me [Jesus] very little things, day by day, as they arise, and by leaving them to me. This was also the way of my priest, Don Dolindo. 'Jesus,' he used to say to me, 'you take care of this.' And then he went on his way lighthearted and confident that I would honor the confidence he placed in me."

Try taking small vacations from worry. Drop off your cares with Jesus for the afternoon. Keep in mind, they're not like your children; you don't have to pick them up again! But if you do, don't be discouraged. Just plan to take another vacation — soon. And you'll get there. *God* will get you there.

Having a surrendered heart is the desired disposition of a contemplative soul. By bringing about a detachment from our selfish clinging and a deep experience of the love of Christ, surrender fulfills the two goals of the contemplative life: purity of heart and an experience of the divine presence within.

Our Blessed Mother Mary is a perfect model of the surrendered life, just as she lived with perfection all the contemplative practices we've explored in this book. That's why I can think of no better way to end our journey than to turn to this unique icon of a contemplative heart: our mother, Mary.

Make It Your Own

Ponder: Consider that our Lord who is all Love and all-powerful is unceasingly and actively involved in caring for you and every detail of your life with thoughtful, tender affection. Know that the more you willingly surrender to him, the greater will be your peace. It's the things we *don't* give to God that plague us.

Pray: "Dear Jesus, please make me willing to surrender my whole life to you. Help me to know you better so I will trust you more. And take away any fear that might be preventing me from putting my life completely in your hands." Then, as anxieties arise, pray the prayer that is repeated throughout the Surrender Novena, given to us by Servant of God Dolindo Ruotolo: "Jesus, I surrender myself to you, take care of everything." (I highly recommend looking up, or buying a copy of, the whole novena.)

Practice: Think of one thing that troubles you and entrust it to Jesus today. Grow in trust through prayerful spiritual reading on the subject of surrender. Some suggestions: *Searching for and Maintaining Peace* by Fr. Jacques Philippe; *Into Your Hands, Father,* by Wilfrid Stinissen; *I Believe in Love,* by Fr. Jean D'Elbee; and anything by Fr. Jean Pierre de Caussade.

Chapter 9

Icon of a Contemplative Heart

"Mary kept all these things, pondering them in her heart."
— Luke 2:19

When you want to reach a goal, it's essential to keep your eyes on the prize — to have before you a vision of what you hope will be the culmination of your quest. The vision directs your steps and keeps you on track. This principle applies not only to secular pursuits, but also to the spiritual venture of cultivating a contemplative heart.

But how can we keep before our eyes the vision of a perfect contemplative heart? By looking at Mary, the icon of contemplative life. Mary embodies, in one human person,[†] what it means to have a contemplative heart — including all the characteristics we've discussed in this book.

So, let's take Mary, queen and mother of contemplatives, as our model and guide. Our meditation on Mary's heart will, of necessity, be a brief sketch, capturing only the outlines of her contemplative image. But hopefully, it will inspire us to want to see her more fully.

Our examination will also serve as a mini digest of the book as we review contemplative characteristics from each chapter in the light of Mary's example. You'll notice I've combined the topics of Chapters 4 and 5 — the value of prayer and the hidden life — together in one section, and similarly, those of Chapters 7 and 8 — suffering and surrender — because they are so closely related. Supported by the presence and intercession of our Mother Mary and the grace of God, we can make these truths, and all those we've learned in this book, our own.

Mary Remembers Jesus

We know from Chapter 1 that "remembering," in the context of the spiritual life, means much more than remembering where we put our keys. Spiritual remembering is an inner *turning toward.* It's a gift of attention, reflection, and caring — a gift of self, offered to God. It may be a quick glance or a lingering look, but always it conveys love. And when you turn toward Jesus, you'll discover he's already looking at you — remembering you — with great tenderness.

Loving remembrance expresses the personal devotion to Jesus that is the driving force and essence of a contemplative soul. And because so many forget him, remembering is also reparation. We're remembering for those who forget. When we remember him, we console his wounded heart. Imagine with what

† Jesus is a *divine* Person, with a human and divine nature.

devotion Mary thought of her son. Could she ever forget him?

In the Rosary, Our Lady invites us into her own prayer of remembrance. She teaches us to ponder and keep within us the mysteries of the life of Jesus as she did and does. With lingering, loving attentiveness, she waited for the Holy Spirit to open up the secrets of the heart of her son. Mary can teach us to wait, to listen, and to reverently receive the treasures of Jesus' life this way.

When we deliberately practice remembering Jesus, it will eventually become an interior habit that we experience as an abiding sense of his presence, as no doubt it was for Mary. Amid many tasks, our hearts can say to the Lord: "In my noisiest hour, there whispers still the ceaseless love of thee." This living awareness of God's presence is integral to the contemplative call.

Our Lady also teaches us to remember the great things God has done for us, and in this way, to glorify him. Like Mary, we can remember these things with praise and thanks. Remembering is a path to intimacy with God, so let's ask our mother to help us improve our memory — especially for the person and wonders of Jesus Christ.

Mary Loves Truth

Truth is a necessity for the contemplative life. Contemplation can in fact be defined as an attentive, loving gaze *on truth.* Here, again, Mary is our forerunner and prototype, for her life was completely formed by, and conformed to, the fullness of Truth in the person of her beloved Son.

Think of Mary's relationship with God. Her Father is the Source of Truth. Her son *is* the Truth. And her Spouse is the Spirit of Truth. Within her dwells the Trinity of Truth. Without doubt, Mary is passionately in love with the Truth, and she calls each of us to this same love.

This love of truth stands in stark contrast to the position

that "truth" is subjective, a matter of personal viewpoint and desire. This subjective version of "truth" is simply a way to serve ourselves.

For Mary, truth was not subjective. She not only believed in objective Truth, she knew him as an objective reality. She saw him, heard him, held him. He who is Being itself and the source of all being is not determined by anyone's opinion, no matter how highly educated. He *is* who he is (see Ex 3:14): eternal, unchanging Truth. Mary's witness speaks loud and clear: Truth is real, and he is worth obeying and loving, living, and dying for.

Although finding truth can be difficult in our world with so many voices clamoring for our attention — from social media "influencers" to political pundits to television evangelists — our Lord promises that everyone who seeks will find (see Mt 7:8). All who truly desire truth and seek it sincerely will find it.

Being perfectly just, our Lord would not ask us to follow the truth without giving us a way to know it. And Jesus is that way. With definite purpose, he gave his word and his authority to the apostles, those men he personally appointed to lead the Church he founded — the Catholic Church. This Church that continues to be led by the direct successors of the apostles is with us today, and it is here that we can find the pure, spiritual truth of God, guarded by the promise of Jesus and the power of the Holy Spirit.

If, like Mary, we are willing to do the will of God, we will be able to recognize the truth (see Jn 7:7). Personal agendas can blind us to truth, but Mary shows us that a surrendered heart is a discerning heart. Because Mary's heart was submitted to the will of God, her ears were open to hear the truth.

Mary Listens to God's Voice

From Genesis through Revelation, Scripture is replete with examples of God speaking to his people. As a logical response, God's word explicitly commands us *to listen to the voice of God* (see Ex 30:20; Ps 95:7). So important is this communication with our Lord that when Mary Magdalene sat at Jesus' feet and "listened to his teaching" (Lk 10:39), he commended her for doing the "one thing" that is "needful" (10:42). Where does listening to God fall on our list of priorities?

Mother Mary, who from the first instant of her life was free from sin and filled with grace, had to have known the voice of God even before she received the message of Gabriel telling her she would be the mother of the Son of God. We can safely assume that, as with the angelic announcement, she treasured, pondered, and ultimately obeyed all the words she received from God. Being the contemplative par excellence, she must also have been proficient in hearing God in the silence, which is filled with his presence.

You, too, can hear and understand the languages of God as he speaks through his word, through the Church, through the circumstances and happenings of your life, through the inner movements of your heart, and even in silence. Mary, instructed as she was by her Spouse, the Holy Spirit, must have been fluent in all these languages. And she's ready to help us learn to hear the voice of God as she did.

Ask Mary, then, to attune your inner ear to God's voice, and to lead you into the deepest form of communication: contemplative silence. Through her intercession, you will be given "ears to hear" the heart of Jesus.

Mary's Hidden Life of Prayer

With sharp insight, Fr. Donald Calloway comments in his book *Consecration to St. Joseph*: "In many ways, the home of the Holy Family in Nazareth was the first Christian monastery." The life of a monastery is a hidden life of prayer and work — *ora et labora*, as stated in the Rule of St. Benedict. This was the life of the Holy Family during Jesus' hidden years: a seamless garment of prayer and work, each interpenetrating the other, accomplished in order and peace in the hiddenness of ordinary life.

This also describes the life of contemplatives in the world: We are hidden in plain sight. For those called to the cloister, the enclosure is a necessary part of their vocation. But not all contemplatives are found in monasteries. Contemplatives who live in the world reside in the enclosure of the heart, the inner person where God dwells. You might remember St. Catherine of Siena referred to this interior enclosure as the "cell" of her heart, that inner sanctuary where she met with Jesus. Whether one lives behind monastery walls or out in the world, it is this *enclosure of the heart* that truly makes a contemplative. Cultivating within your soul a silent, sheltered, sacred meeting place for you and Jesus, a spiritual "house of prayer," is the essence of contemplative life and the source of its joy.

Mary knew this. Even while going through her daily tasks, there arose from her heart the holy incense of prayer offered in love. What transforming power, what eternal worth flowed through her humdrum days! Remember what makes such apparent "nothings" valuable: love, divine love that is received from God and is offered back to him.

Before Saint Paul wrote his first letter to the Corinthians, before Saint Thérèse discovered her Little Way centuries later, Mary knew that love is the "more excellent way" (1 Cor 12:31). Divine love is more powerful, more effective, more precious in the eyes of God than all other ministries and gifts combined. To pray with love, to work with love (no matter how menial the task), *to be love*: There is nothing greater.

Mary didn't seek to be ranked among the apostles. She didn't covet a high position in the Church. She was a pure, living flame of love. What else was there? What more could she want?

Contemplative prayer feeds this divine love in our souls. That's why contemplatives — and, in fact, all of us in our contemplation — are the spiritual heart of the Body of Christ, pumping the vivifying power of love to all his members. You don't have to be physically present to touch the lives of others. With prayer and love, you can reach everywhere, from anywhere. Mary did just that, and from heaven, she is still doing it.

Whatever your call, public or private, you can preserve the hidden life of love within by guarding your prayer life and seeking to emulate the interior dispositions of Mary. Fr. Livio Fanzaga encourages us: "Seek to be a living image of the very humble one, who never put herself on display and who knows how to pass through the world unknown, she who is the greatest of all creatures. Work solely for love of God, love being an ordinary person. … You will then be a flower that Mary cultivates in this world of external appearances. Her scent will reawaken in the hearts of men a nostalgia for being little and humble."

Sr. Ruth Borrows writes in her book *Through Him, With Him, In Him: Meditations on the Liturgical Seasons*, "To live a contemplative life is to live at depth; to live below the surface in the world of faith, the world of reality, and not appearances." No one models this better than Mary, and she shows through her humble example that this beautiful inner life is meant for *you*.

Mary, Spouse of God

In Chapter 6, we explored the reality that each of us, whether in religious or lay life, is called to be a spouse of Christ. Holiness is not two-tiered: one level for priests and religious and a lower level for laypeople. We are all called to the summit of sanctity. Understanding this truth is of the utmost importance to every Christian, because we will not seek the fullness of holiness if we believe it's not meant for us. Instead, we will accept spiritual mediocrity and, as a result, never fulfill God's will for our lives. This is not what God wants for us. Mary's life makes this clear.

Mary is the holiest human person who ever lived, or ever

will live. (Remember, Jesus is a *divine* Person with a human and a divine nature.) Mary lived the perfection of charity in fullness and purity. No one loved God with a more sacrificial, wholehearted love. She gave herself totally to God, holding back not even the slightest particle of her being. She was (and still is) the intimate spouse of God the Holy Spirit. And she was a laywoman — a married laywoman.

Just in case anyone should doubt that Mary and Joseph were truly married, we have the assurance of the Church, which teaches that the marriage of Mary and Joseph was a real marriage. Notice that even in the Eucharistic canons of the Mass, Saint Joseph is referred to as Mary's "spouse."

St. Peter Julian Eymard explains: "Mary belonged to Joseph, and Joseph to Mary, so much so, that their marriage was very real, since they gave themselves to each other. But how could they do this? They reciprocally gave their virginity, and over this virginity they gave themselves a mutual right. What right? To safeguard the other's virtue." What's more, as Fr. Donald Calloway writes in his book *Consecration to St. Joseph*, "Trusting in God's plan, [Mary] fell in love with St. Joseph and gave him her heart."

And yet, she still loved God with her *whole* heart. We see, through Mary's life, that one love does not exclude the other — just the opposite. It was by following her God-given vocation to marriage and motherhood that Mary reached the peak of holiness and the fullness of love intended for her by God from eternity.

If the heights of holiness aren't open to laypeople, Mary's life is certainly sending the wrong message. But, of course, it isn't. In fact, the Church points to Mary as the preeminent example, second only to Jesus, for every Christian. Her life is our lesson. And it's teaching us that each one of us is indeed called to the fullness of holiness, and that there's nothing higher, holier, or greater than doing God's will by living out our vocation, whatever it may be.

Recall how, in *Christifideles Laici*, Pope St. John Paul II states this very thing: "Everyone in the Church, precisely because they are members, receive and thereby share in the common vocation to holiness. In the fullness of this title and on equal par with all other members of the Church, the lay faithful are called to holiness: 'All the faithful of Christ of whatever rank or status are called to the fullness of Christian life and to the perfection of charity.'"

These are the words of a pope, a saint, and an ecumenical council of the Church. And they echo the words of Jesus, who commands each of us to love God with our whole heart, to renounce all for love of him, to be perfect as our heavenly Father is perfect — *and* who identifies himself as the Bridegroom of the Church. (That includes you and me.)

Mary taught us through her life that, as St. Teresa Benedicta of the Cross expressed it, "With the utmost tender love will [Jesus] seek to win every single one as bride."

Mary's Suffering and Surrender

In Chapter 7, we saw that sharing the cross of Jesus is an essential part of the contemplative call. Through this union with Christ crucified, we become open portals for the grace of his redeeming sacrifice to flow into the world.

And while no human being can participate completely in the sufferings of Christ, no one shared more completely in his cross than Mary. That's why the Church calls her Queen of Martyrs. True, she didn't physically die when Jesus was crucified, but is it easier to suffer the pains of death and *die,* or to suffer the pains of death and *go on living*? Is it harder for a mother to suffer, or to watch her child suffer? While Mary didn't bear nail prints in her hands, the Church has traditionally believed that "every pain in [Jesus'] body had a corresponding echo in her heart," as

Fr. Wilfrid Stinissen expresses it in his book *Mary in the Bible and in Our Lives.*

Mary's suffering wasn't limited to the time of the crucifixion. It punctuated her life, from the uncertainty of what bearing the "Son of the Most High" (Lk 1:32) would mean, to the rigors and anxiety of traveling to Bethlehem with child, to the prophecy of Simeon, to losing Jesus for three days when he was twelve years old, to the annoyances of daily life.

To appreciate more deeply how Mary bore her suffering and lived her surrender, let's look at how she lived the lessons laid out in Chapter 7. Through her, may we learn to suffer and not lose faith, to trust even when God's plan seems to make no sense, and to carry our cross as a contemplative: living in the presence of God, steeped in prayer.

- **Contemplative preparation:** Mary's whole life prepared her for the cross. She lived with an awareness of God's presence, even if, at times, it was an awareness based solely on faith. She pondered God's word in the temple of her heart where there arose a continual silent offering of love and intercession. This ongoing contact with God filled her soul with "his glorious might" (Col 1:11). And this is where we must begin as well, drawing our life and our strength from prayer and God's presence. For Scripture tells us that "in [his] presence" we find "fullness of joy" (Ps 16:11), the joy that is our strength (Neh 8:10).
- **Paradox of power:** Mary also recognized and rejoiced in the spiritual significance of littleness and hiddenness. She saw herself as God's lowly handmaid, so much so that she was startled and troubled (see Lk 1:29) by the thought that God wanted to use

her to do great things. Yet, after being convinced by the archangel Gabriel, she rejoiced that God chooses the little ones (Lk 1:47–48).

Mary is the exquisite example of God's power being made perfect in weakness. Her poverty made room for his majesty. Her humility made her a fit instrument of his might. God chose the littlest one to bring the greatest One, his Son, into the world. And he still prefers to work through "nobodies." If you're weak, without great power or influence, one of those the world overlooks, rejoice with Mary! God wants to use *you* to bring Jesus into the world. Your infirmities and weaknesses are no hindrance to him. On the contrary, they make room for his action. God does great things because *he* is mighty, not because you are. Let Mary's life give you hope and convince you that this is true.

- **The principle of faith:** Mary believed the amazing promises she received from God through the archangel Gabriel. Her son would be the Son of God and have a kingdom that would never end. But her faith was tested when she saw before her eyes a beaten, bloody King, crowned with thorns by those who hated him, dying before it seemed his kingdom could begin. And yet she continued to believe. She didn't allow what she didn't know (or understand) to cause her to lose what she did know. Her son was the Son of God. Gabriel's word would prove true. She didn't have to know how. She kept her faith; she *stood*; and she saw, with the eyes of faith, the kingdom of God coming in power. If she could, by God's grace, keep her faith in such circumstances, she can help us to do the same in our trials.

- **Sovereignty of God:** Mary believed that God was sovereign over her life, even over the power of Rome. Her Almighty Father would bring good out of evil, even the ultimate evil of the death of her son. She had witnessed her Father's hand weaving the threads of her life, guiding, providing, arranging all things. She was confident he would use even hindrances and opposition to advance his plan. Everything would be turned, not only to the fulfillment of her deepest desires, but to the advantage of the whole world. Her part was to continue to live her "yes" with faith. We can see in hindsight that Mary's trust in the sovereignty and providence of God was justified. He drew unimaginable good out of evil, and he will do it in our lives, too.
- **Knowing God:** Mary's strength came through her relationship with the Father, Son, and Holy Spirit. She knew she was the beloved daughter of the Father. Her son was the joy and light of her life. And the love of the Holy Spirit gave her comfort and fortitude. She *knew* in whom she believed, and she knew she could trust him. This experiential knowledge of God gave her a steadfast inner stability. With Mary, we too, through our encounters with God, can develop a confidence in him that nothing can shake because we *know him.*
- **Goodwill and surrender:** Jesus said, "No one takes [my life] from me, but I lay it down of my own accord" (Jn 10:18). For love of the Father and love of us, Jesus freely chose to lay down his life. It appeared to be stolen from him by hostile forces, but interiorly, he had already given his life (explicitly on Holy Thursday). The same could be said of Mary. She

had already freely given her life to God. She chose to will his will (the definition of goodwill), whatever it might bring.

Mary's son wasn't wrested from her grasp. Following Jesus' example, she willingly offered him for love of the Father and Son, and for love of us. Says Fr. Wilfrid Stinissen: "Mary stood near the Cross like a priest who celebrates Mass: she offered her son to the Father. The Son whom the Father gave into her hands, she gave back freely." Further: "Mary was not used as a purely passive instrument; rather, she cooperated with her faith and obedience in the salvation of mankind."

And we can be sure that as Jesus forgave his persecutors, Mary, following his example, forgave. So must we, with God's grace, forgive those who hurt us. Our Mother Mary will help us.

Mary's example teaches us not to endure our trials like a stoic, gritting our teeth, stifling our complaints, but instead to freely choose God's will, for love of him and others. This self-sacrificing love is the source of joy, a joy even suffering can't extinguish. St. Francis of Assisi bore the wounds of Christ, and yet he is known as the saint of joy. So don't be surprised if, when you freely offer your life to God anticipating only suffering, you find joy.

Is It Possible?

Looking at Mary, we see the pristine beauty of her contemplative heart. Then we look at ourselves — our weak, inconstant, stumbling selves. And we wonder how it could be possible that God is calling us to have a contemplative heart like Mary's, to have a holy heart filled with his love. We can't help but ask: "How can this be? You know me, Lord."

Wasn't that Mary's question? "How can this be?" (Lk 1:34). And what was the answer? "With God nothing will be impossible" (1:37). And that's God's answer to us, too. Like Mary, God has also given us a promise, through the lips of Saint Paul, which he's asking us to believe: "May the God of peace himself sanctify you wholly; and may your spirit and soul and body be kept sound and blameless at the coming of our Lord Jesus Christ. He who calls you is faithful, and he will do it" (1 Thes 5:23–24).

God has promised to give you a holy heart, a contemplative heart. *He will do it.* If you're willing, if you desire it, if you, like Mary, say, "Let it be to me according to your word" (Lk 1:38).

Make It Your Own

Ponder: Mary's life is your promise. In her, God is showing you what he desires to do in you. But Mary is more than a model; she's a mother. Your mother. She loves you tenderly, personally. With the Holy Spirit, she will gently fashion within you another Bethany, a place where Jesus is welcomed and loved, listened to, and consoled. A place of intimate friendship and abiding joy for you and your Beloved. In Mary, God has given you both the vision and the loving help you need to be a contemplative in the world. You are not alone. Your mother's love is constant and unstoppable.

Pray: When was the last time you talked to Mary? Our relationship with Jesus suffers when we forget he is a real Person who is present to us right here, right now. The same can be said about our relationship with Mother Mary. Speak to her from your heart. She's listening. Tell her honestly whatever is on your mind. Entrust to her your cares and hopes.

Practice: Take some time to leisurely pray two decades of the Rosary in the contemplative spirit of Mary, treasuring and reflecting upon the mysteries of Jesus' life. I like to think of holding the Rosary as putting my hand in Mary's. Ask the Holy Spirit to conform your heart to Mary's contemplative heart. Who knows? One day you might hear the Father say, "You look like your Mom." Finally, consider consecrating your life to the Immaculate Heart of Mary. (I recommend Fr. Michael Gaitley's book *33 Days to Morning Glory* as an accessible and fruitful way of making this consecration. There are also the excellent classic writings of St. Louis de Montfort.) If you want to belong to Jesus, belong to Mary. For she will keep you close to her son and teach you to "do whatever he tells you" (Jn 2:5) — with love.

A Parting Prayer

When we began our contemplative journey, I said that there's nothing more important you could do with your life than cultivating a contemplative heart, a heart in love with God. I hope now you can see more clearly why that's true.

To send you on your way, let me pray a short prayer for each one of you. I pray "that Christ may dwell in your hearts through faith; that you, being rooted and grounded in love, may have power to comprehend with all the saints what is the breadth and length and height and depth, and to know the love of Christ which surpasses knowledge, that you may be filled with all the fullness of God" (Eph 3:17–19). God bless you!

Acknowledgments

I would like to thank Mike Aquilina for his kindness and encouragement, and for pointing me in the right direction. I would also like to thank Jaymie Stuart Wolfe for taking the time to share her writing wisdom, which helped me to see the book in a new way. I am deeply grateful for Mary Beth Giltner, my editor. Then there's Fr. John Victoria, who suggested that I put the whole project into the hands of Saint Joseph. I must also express my immeasurable appreciation for my late spiritual director, Fr. Leo McKernan, who played a key role in helping me to recognize and follow my contemplative call. Finally, I want to thank my husband, Stan, my excellent "in-house" editor, and the family and friends who have supported me with their prayers and encouragement. God bless each one of you!

Works Cited

Altier, Fr. Robert J. *God's Plan for Your Marriage: An Exploration of Holy Matrimony from Genesis to the Wedding Feast of the Lamb.* Sophia Institute Press, 2022.

Antonellis, Rev. Costanzo J., C.S.S.R. *A Saint of Ardent Desires: Meditations on the Virtues of St. Thérèse of Lisieux.* Daughters of St. Paul, 1965.

Augustine, Saint. *Enchiridion de Fide, Spe et Caritate,* no. 24. Quoted in Wilfrid Stinissen. *Into your Hands, Father: Abandoning Ourselves to the God Who Loves Us.* Ignatius Press, 2011.

Benedict XVI, Pope. *The Yes of Jesus Christ: Exercises in Faith, Hope, and Love.* Translated by Robert Newell. Augustinian Heritage Institute, 1992.

Benedictine monk. *In Sinu Jesu: When Heart Speaks to Heart.* Angelico Press, 2016.

Bossis, Gabrielle. *He and I.* Pauline Books and Media, 2016.

Brother Andrew. *God's Smuggler.* The Penguin Group, 1967.

Brother Lawrence. *The Practice of the Presence of God.* Paraclete Press, 2010.

Bunel, Pere Jacques. *Listen to the Silence: A Retreat with Pere Jacques.* Translated and edited by Francis J. Murphy. ICS Publications, 2005.

Burrows, Sister Ruth, OCD. *Through Him, With Him, In Him: Meditations on the Liturgical Seasons*. Sheed and Ward, 1987.

Calloway, Donald H., MIC. *Consecration to St. Joseph: The Wonders of Our Spiritual Father*. Marian Press, 2020.

De Caussade, Fr. Jean-Pierre, SJ. *Abandonment to Divine Providence*. Translated by John Beevers. Doubleday, 1975.

De Caussade, Fr. Jean-Pierre, SJ. *The Spiritual Letters of Father P. J. de Caussade, SJ*. Translated by Algar Thorold. Burns, Oates & Washbourne Ltd., 1934.

Davidson, Fr. Sean. *Saint Mary Magdalene: Prophetess of Eucharistic Love*. Ignatius Press, 2017.

D'Elbee, Pere Jean du Coeur de Jesus. *I Believe in Love: Retreat Conferences on the Interior Life*. Translated by Marilyn Teichert and Madeleine Stebbins. St. Bede's Publications, 1974.

Dubay, Fr. Thomas. *Seeking Spiritual Direction: How to Grow the Divine Life Within*. Servant Publications, 1993.

Fanzaga, Livio. *The Deceiver: Our Daily Struggle with Satan*. Sugarco Edizioni. English copyright by Roman Catholic Books, 2000.

St. Faustina Kowalska. *Divine Mercy in My Soul - Diary*. Marian Press, 1987.

Gaitley, Fr. Michael E. *33 Days to Morning Glory: A Do-It-Yourself Retreat in Preparation for Marian Consecration*. Marian Press, 2011.

Gallagher, Timothy M., OMV. *The Discernment of Spirits: An Ignatian Guide for Everyday Living*. Crossroad Publishing Company, 2005.

Giertych, Fr. Wojciech, OP. *The Spark of Faith: Understanding the Power of Reaching Out to God*. EWTN Publishing, 2018.

Guillerand, Dom Augustin. *The Prayer of the Presence of God*. Sophia Institute Press, 2005.

Haggerty, Fr. Donald. *The Contemplative Hunger*. Ignatius Press, 2016.

Haggerty, Fr. Donald. *Contemplative Provocations*. Ignatius Press, 2013.

Hoffman, Dominic M., OP. *The Life Within: The Prayer of Union*. Sheed and Ward, 1966.

John Paul II, Pope. *The Lay Members of Christ's Faithful People: Christifideles Laici*. Pauline Books and Media, 1989.

John-Terry, Chris. *The Secret of the Saints*. Alba House Publishers, 1999.

Marie-Eugene of the Child Jesus, OCD. *Under the Torrent of His Love: Thérèse of Lisieux, A Spiritual Genius*. Translated by Sr. Mary Thomas Noble, OP. Alba House Publishers, 1995.

Marie-Eugene of the Child Jesus, OCD. *Where the Spirit Breathes: Prayer and Action*. Translated by Sr. Mary Thomas Noble, OP. Alba House Publishers, 1998.

Martínez, Luis Maria. *Only Jesus*. Translated by Sr. Mary St. Daniel. Cluny Media, 2020.

McKenna, Sr. Briege, OSC, with Henry Libersat. *Miracles Do Happen: God Can Do the Impossible*. Servant Books, 1987.

Moorecroft, Jennifer. *He Is My Heaven: The Life of Elizabeth of the Trinity*. ICS Publications, 2001.

Mother Mary Francis, PC. *A Right to Be Merry*. All Saints Press, 1965.

Nycander, Maud, dir. *The Nun: The Story of a Carmelite Vocation*. Ignatius Press, 2010. DVD, 60 minutes.

Philippe, Fr. Jacques. *Searching for and Maintaining Peace: A Small Treatise on Peace of Heart*. Translated by George and Jannie Driscoll. Alba House Publishers, 2002.

Philippe, Fr. Jacques. *Thirsting for Prayer*. Scepter Publishers, Inc., 2014.

Philippe, Fr. Jacques. *Time for God: A Guide to Prayer*. Translated by Helen Scott. Scepter Publishers, Inc., 1992.

Rosewell Moore, Pamela. *The Five Silent Years of Corrie ten Boom*. Zondervan Publishing House, 1986.

Sales, Lorenzo, IMC. *Jesus Appeals to the World: From the Writings of Sr. Consolata Betrone*. Alba House Publishers, 1955.

Scanlan, Fr. Michael, TOR, with James Manney. *What Does God Want? A Practical Guide to Making Decisions*. Our Sunday Visitor Publishing Division, 1996.

Schryvers, Rev. Joseph, C.SS.R. *The Gift of Oneself: Surrendering Oneself to God as a Way of Life*. TAN Books and Publishers, Inc., 1934.

Stinissen, Fr. Wilfrid. *Into Your Hands, Father: Abandoning Ourselves to the God Who Loves Us*. Translated by Sr. Clare Maire, OCD. Ignatius Press, 2011.

Stinissen, Fr. Wilfrid. *Mary in the Bible and in Our Lives*. Translated by Sr. Clare Marie, OCD. Ignatius Press, 2018.

St. Teresa Benedicta of the Cross. *Collected Works of Edith Stein, Vol. Six*. Translated by Josephine Koeppel, OCD. ICS Publications, 2002.

St. Thérèse of Lisieux. *Story of a Soul: The Autobiography of St. Thérèse of Lisieux*. Edited by Mother Agnes of Jesus, translated by Michael Day. Sourcebooks.

Thomas, Mother Catherine. *My Beloved: The Story of a Carmelite Nun*. Doubleday and Co., 1955.

Voillaume, Rene. *Seeds in the Desert: Like Jesus of Nazareth*. Translated and adapted by Willard Hill. Fides Publishers, Inc., 1964.

About the Author

Mary Beth Kremski returned to the Catholic Church, after several years in Protestantism, with a new-found faith in Catholicism and a great love for the Church. Through the autobiography of St. Thérèse of Lisieux, she discovered contemplative spirituality and knew she had found her spiritual path. Since then, she has sought to learn more deeply what it means to have a contemplative heart and uses her writing to share this knowledge with others. She has written for several Catholic publications and contributed her story to the book *Surprised by Truth 2*, as well as having appeared on Catholic radio and television. She writes from Pennsylvania, where she lives with her husband, Stan.